HAUNTED CASTLES OF
BRITAIN AND IRELAND

HAUNTED
CASTLES OF
BRITAIN AND IRELAND

RICHARD JONES

with photographs by

JOHN MASON

NEW HOLLAND

First published in 2003 by New Holland Publishers (UK) Ltd
London • Cape Town • Sydney • Auckland

10 9 8 7 6 5 4 3 2

Garfield House, 86-88 Edgware Road, London W2 2EA,
United Kingdom
www.newhollandpublishers.com

80 McKenzie Street, Cape Town 8001,
South Africa

Level 1/Unit 4, 14 Aquatic Drive, Frenchs Forest, NSW 2086,
Australia

218 Lake Road, Northcote, Auckland,
New Zealand

ISBN 1 84330 436 8

Publishing Manager: Jo Hemmings
Project Editor: Lorna Sharrock
Copy Editor: Sue Viccars
Designer: Gülen Shevki
Cartographer: Bill Smuts
Index: Janet Dudley
Production: Lucy Hulme

Front cover: Bamburgh Castle
Back cover: Ruthin Castle
Page 1: Farnham Castle; Pages 2–3: Charleville Forest Castle
Pages 4–5: Ludlow Castle; Pages 6–7: Main picture: Dunottar
Castle; From left to right: Sherborne Old Castle, Lydford Castle,
Raglan Castle, Eilean Donan Castle, Ruthin Castle;
Page 160: Carisbrooke Castle.

Reproduction by Pica Digital Pte Ltd, Singapore
Printed and bound in Singapore by Kyodo Printing Co
(Singapore) Pte Ltd

KEY TO SITE SYMBOLS

NATIONAL TRUST	✿
ENGLISH HERITAGE	Ⓔ
BED AND BREAKFAST	⛱
ADMISSION CHARGE	Ⓐ
CAN ONLY VISIT ON A TOUR	Ⓣ
RUIN	Ⓡ

Even Such is Time, which takes in trust
Our youth, our joys, and all we have,
And pays us but with age and dust;
Who in the dark and silent grave,
When we have wandered all our ways,
Shuts up the story of our days:
And from which earth, and grave, and dust,
The Lord shall raise me up, I trust.

EPITAPH

BY SIR WALTER RALEGH (1552–1618)

CONTENTS

INTRODUCTION

 It has been said that ghosts appear only in houses that have known great happiness or great misery. The castles of Britain and Ireland fall into both categories. Many owners must have gazed with enormous pride upon the soaring walls of their newly built strongholds. Births, marriages and victory celebrations must have been joyous occasions during which the walls and chambers of many a formidable bastion echoed to the sound of merrymaking. But there was also a darker side to the picture, for castles were built for defence. The majority were intended as tools of subjugation and were viewed with revulsion by many who lived under the yoke of oppression. During times of war, the lord, his family and their garrison would retreat into their castle and attempt to repel their enemies. We can only guess at the feelings of fear and horror that must have hung over a castle during a siege. If happiness and misery do indeed bring ghosts back to a building, then the castles of Britain and Ireland have almost a thousand years of such emotions crackling within their ancient fabrics.

The pages that follow are the result of a journey I undertook around Britain and Ireland over a period of eleven months. I visited close on 200 castles, soaking up their atmosphere and researching their ghost stories. I was conscious that it would be easy to end up with a nebulous

OPPOSITE: The austere lines of the 14th-century Bodiam Castle – a superb example of medieval military architecture – is mirrored in the gleaming moat.

BELOW: The ragged remnants of Sanquhar Castle in Dumfries and Galloway once gave up the secret of an ancient murder.

LEFT: Charville Forest Castle was Ireland's first Gothic Revival castle, completed in the early 19th century, and appropriately gothic-style spirits have moved in.

OPPOSITE: Sherbourne Old Castle in Dorset is blighted by an ancient curse that has brought misery into the lives of many of its past owners.

The two questions I am most often asked as I go about my researches are, 'Do you believe in ghosts?' and 'Have you ever seen a ghost?' I have spoken with too many sober and publicity-shy people who have seen ghosts not to believe in them, but I am not convinced that they are the dead returning to haunt the living. Indeed, the more I explore supernatural phenomena, the more I become convinced that hauntings are the result of a strong emotion that has somehow become recorded on its surroundings and simply awaits the right person to come along and press 'Play'. I have never to my knowledge actually seen a ghost. Indeed, very few people do see ghosts: they feel, smell, hear and sense them but a full manifestation is very rare. I have certainly experienced and heard things that I have been unable to explain, and visited places where I have felt decidedly uneasy. I found Rait Castle in Scotland truly terrifying, although quite why, I don't know. Charleville Forest, Huntingdon and Leap Castles in Ireland; Balgonie and Fyvie Castles in Scotland; and Chillingham Castle in England; are all places I would encourage all who seek mysterious encounters to visit.

stream of white, pink, blue and green ladies parading across the pages of the book, so I attempted to uncover, wherever possible, the stories behind the castles and their hauntings. I attempted to include castles that would present my readers with a variety of hauntings and locations. I didn't want the book to be just a trawl through castle ruins, but for it to uncover places that are lived in today, as well as those where readers could, if they so desired, spend the night. The most important criterion for inclusion was that my readers must be able to visit the castles. Thus every castle included is open to the public as an attraction, museum or hotel.

I hope you enjoy reading this book as much as I have enjoyed researching it, and I hope you will explore the castles. Should you happen to be in the right place at the right time, and become one of the lucky few who has witnessed a ghost, please feel free to share your experience with me.

RICHARD JONES
www.Haunted-Britain.com

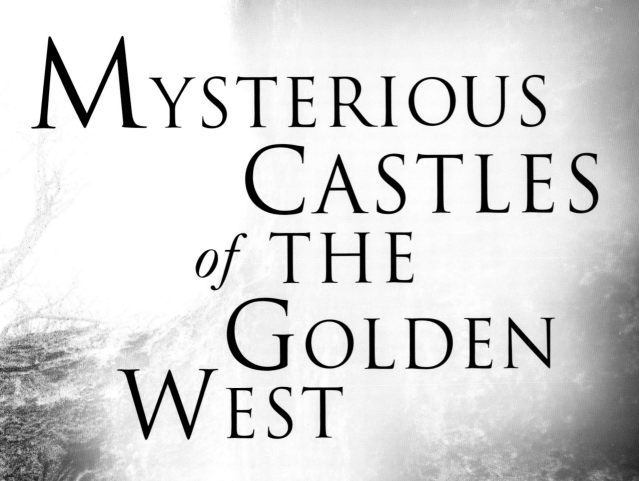

MYSTERIOUS CASTLES of THE GOLDEN WEST

A shadow flits before me
Not thou, but like to thee:
Ah Christ that it was possible
For one short hour to see
The souls we loved, that they might tell us
What and where they be.

FROM MAUD
BY ALFRED, LORD TENNYSON (1809–92)

CORNWALL, DEVON & SOMERSET

Engﾠland's West Country possesses a singular aura of mysterious enchantment, and nowhere is this more apparent than in the castles that stud its magical landscape. There are crumbling vestiges, steeped in legend and imbued with the chivalric spirit of King Arthur and the enigmatic Merlin. There are mighty strongholds, built by powerful Norman nobles, from which past residents seem both unable and unwilling to depart. There are sturdy, fortress-like homes, upon the very fabric of which successive generations of great and powerful families have left indelible psychic imprints. Every so often, these blink into life and provide astonished onlookers with spectral re-enactments of some long-ago happening. Many sad and fascinating tales lie behind these hauntings. Wicked spouses, fickle lovers, evil squires and gross miscarriages of justice abound, and provide glimpses into a past when this was an isolated area, far removed from the refinements of civilized society. Add to this the tangible remains of nearly 5,000 years of history and you begin to realize how this region still has the ability to draw visitors from all over the world.

KEY

1. Pengersick Castle
2. Lydford Castle
3. Okehampton Castle
4. Berry Pomeroy Castle
5. Powderham Castle
6. Tiverton Castle
7. Taunton Castle
8. Dunster Castle
9. Farleigh Hungerford Castle

PENGERSICK CASTLE
Praa Sands, Cornwall ①
CORNWALL'S SPOOKIEST CASTLE

A forlorn aura hangs over the picturesque bulk of Pengersick Castle. It is a beautiful and magical place, yet there are parts where you sense an indefinable hopelessness, as though some long-ago tragedy or dastardly deed is about to be re-enacted before you. It comes as little surprise, therefore, to discover that Pengersick (the name means 'the head of a marshy place') is one of the most haunted sites in Cornwall. The family who built the castle took their name from its boggy location, and the original owner, Henry Pengersick, appears to have been something of a psychopath who contributed to the ghostly population of his family home. Ecclesiastical figures featured high on his hate list, and he was excommunicated for killing an innocent monk from Hailes Abbey in Gloucestershire who had the audacity to drop by to collect tithes. Whether the monk is the spectral hooded figure who now wanders the castle and its grounds is uncertain, but he has been spotted many times, especially around the small forest at the end of the medieval garden. Assaulting and murdering churchmen aside, Henry Pengersick was also a man with dynastic ambitions, and he chose as his bride the beautiful Engrina Godolphin, a daughter of the family that owned the adjoining estate. The testosterone-fuelled escapades of her violent husband may well have taken their toll on the gentle Engrina, for her spirit is said to roam the old castle, and has a particular affinity for the main bedroom. This particularly haunted chamber is home to at least two other spirits. In the early hours of some days, guests have been startled by the sudden appearance of a ghostly woman by the window. After a few moments of gazing pensively out onto the night, she turns and walks to the Jacobean four-poster bed. Lying down, she suddenly clutches her stomach and begins writhing in agony. Could she be the earthbound revenant of some former resident who was poisoned in the room? Some say she is, and claim that the other female figure (who appears through the wall to stand by her bedside) is the maid who nursed her through her last agonizing hours. Of course, all this is little more than convenient speculation, for only the walls know the truth — and they are not telling.

There is no doubt that Pengersick Castle merits a visit from all those seeking ghostly encounters, and many who come do not leave disappointed. Whether it be the sight of Alexander, the fearless black cat, chasing spectral rats around the grounds; the white orbs and weird shapes that show up on some photographs but are absent from others taken just seconds later; the demon dog with the fiery red eyes; or even the eerie white mist that writhes

ABOVE: Pengersick Castle, one of the most haunted sites in Cornwall, is home to many spectres including a hooded monk and a demon dog.

towards terrified witnesses; this old place is a castle of secrets where past and present live side by side and every so often can merge with alarming results.

LYDFORD CASTLE
Lydford, Devon Ⓔ
WICKED JUDGE JEFFREYS

Lydford's ancient Norman castle, built in 1195, gives the bizarre impression of having sunk into the mound. Once inside the roofless tower, you can climb down to the now underground level. A cursory glance upwards at the massively thick walls evokes a vivid impression of what a fearsome and intimidating place this must have been when, in the Middle Ages, it was used as both a court of law and a prison. During the reign of Henry VIII, it was described unflatteringly as 'one of the most heinous, contagious and detestable places within the realm', and the castle still evokes cold shivers today. The castle's spectral inhabitant is said to be the dreaded Judge Jeffreys. In the aftermath of the Monmouth Rebellion of 1685, the judge meted out savage retribution on behalf of the soon-to-be-exiled king, James II. At the notorious 'Bloody Assizes,' Jeffreys routed out Monmouth's supporters, and condemned many to the gallows. He held court in many Devonshire towns, and legend holds that he was at his savage and judicial best at Lydford, despite a scarcity of historical evidence that he ever visited the village. Whether or not he did, such was the loathing that his memory inspired in

ABOVE: The infamous Judge Jeffrys, who sent many to their deaths in his 'Bloody Assizes', is said to haunt Lydford Castle in the guise of a hideous black pig.

PREVIOUS PAGES: The hollow shell of the once-splendid mansion of Berry Pomery Castle conceals the dungeon realm of the beautiful 'blue lady', Margaret.

nightly penance whereby she travels across Dartmoor in a carriage made from the bones of her supposed victims and, upon arriving at Okehampton Castle, plucks one blade of grass from the hillside. Only when all the grass is gone will Mary Howard's penance be complete, releasing her from the onerous task with which a blatant case of mistaken identity has burdened her!

BERRY POMEROY CASTLE
Berry Pomeroy, Devon Ⓐ Ⓔ
TRAGIC MOTHER, JEALOUS SISTER

The ancient and powerful Pomeroy family arrived in Devon with the Norman Conquest, although the castle that bears their name dates only from the 15th century.

Legend holds that Edward VI ordered the seizure of their castle as revenge for the family's part in the religious rebellion of 1549. When troops arrived to enforce the order, the two Pomeroy brothers who held the castle donned their armour, blindfolded their horses and spurred them over the ramparts, where they crashed to their deaths at the feet of their astonished would-be captors.

The building was then acquired by the king's Protector, Edward Seymour, and following Seymour's execution in 1552, became the abode of his son, also called Edward. The family extended the building, and added a magnificent manor house. When it was struck by lightning in 1685, they lost interest, and by 1701, the house had become a mouldering ruin.

Today the rambling ruins of the once-mighty fortress perch eerily on a rocky throne above a wooded ravine, and several ghosts are said to wander inside its crumbling walls. A blue lady haunts the hollow shell of the splendid 16th-century manor house. She is said to be a daughter of the Pomeroy family who was impregnated by her own father. She smothered her baby the moment it was born and is condemned to wander the ruins at night in eternal remorse. But the eeriest part of this eeriest of ruins is located beneath the 15th-century Margaret Tower, reached by a twisting stone staircase that spirals down into a dank, dark dungeon, where a feeling of dreadful foreboding emanates from the moss-clad walls. Here

these parts that he has long been said to haunt Lydford and its castle in the guise of huge black pig!

OKEHAMPTON CASTLE
Okehampton, Devon Ⓐ Ⓔ
THE ETERNAL PENITENT
AND THE CARRIAGE OF BONES

Although the history of this early Norman castle, the stark ruins of which cling precariously to a thin shale outcrop, is relatively uneventful, its spectral tenant has a delightfully melodramatic quality to her nocturnal machinations. Mary Howard was a relatively well-to-do lady who, for reasons unknown, chose to disinherit her children. In death, however, she has become confused with Lady Frances Howard – a notorious poisoner (see page 27) – and legend has defamed her memory by attributing to her the murders of four husbands. As a result, she has been condemned to perform a

ABOVE LEFT: Only when she has plucked every blade of grass from the hill on which Okehampton Castle stands will Lady Frances Howard be able to rest in peace.

OPPOSITE ABOVE: As the wind stirs the winter trees that surround Berry Pomery Castle, visitors may encounter the ghost of a daughter who was the tragic victim of lust.

OPPOSITE BELOW: The well-preserved Powderham Castle on the Exe estuary is the haunt of a mysterious lady, often seen strolling between the castle and the local church.

dreadful foreboding emanates from the moss-clad walls. Here the wicked Eleanor Pomeroy imprisoned and starved to death her sister Margaret, because they both loved the same man and she was jealous of her sibling's beauty. Margaret's misty form appears in the depths of the tower, and many visitors have felt the cold chill of her unseen presence as she brushes by them on the dimly lit stairwell that leads to her eternal prison cell.

POWDERHAM CASTLE
Powderham, Devon Ⓐ
WALLED UP ALIVE

Powderham Castle, the ancestral home of the Earl and Countess of Devon, was built in 1379 by Sir Phillip Courtenay, and is one of the oldest family homes in England. Many of the medieval rooms still exist and are inhabited by several former occupants. Two hundred years ago, during renovation work in the Guard Tower, one of the oldest parts, it was discovered that one of the

ancient walls was hollow. Breaking it down, horrified workmen discovered a secret room containing the bones of a woman and a baby. Although the grisly remains were reinterred in Powderham Church, the spirits of the unknown mother and child have remained at the place where, according to several mediums, they were bricked up alive and left to die in cold

years and, in 1495 William Courtenay married Princess Katherine Plantagenet, youngest daughter of Edward IV and sister to the two Princes in the Tower. After this high point, the senior line of the family died out in 1556, and ownership of Tiverton Castle fluctuated between various of William's descendants until it passed to the Giffard family.

Held for the king during the Civil War, the castle was besieged by General Fairfax and was taken in October 1645, when a fortuitous shot struck the drawbridge chain. Thereafter, wealthy wool merchant Peter West, whose daughter married Sir Peter Carew, bought it. Carew's descendants sold the castle in 1923 and after various changes of ownership it was bought in 1960 by Ivar Campbell, whose nephew, Angus, inherited it in 1985.

There are several ghost stories associated with the property. The first dates back to the 17th century when the governor of the castle was Sir Hugh Spencer, a widower, whose 21-year-old daughter Alice was considered one of the great beauties of the district. Alice had many admirers, but her father considered it his duty to ensure she married only the wealthiest of them. He chose as his son-in-law Sir Charles Trevor, an immensely rich man several years Alice's senior, who was renowned both for his violent temper and sour disposition.

The manager of Tiverton Castle, Maurice Fortescue, had fallen in love with the girl, but knowing that her father would never consider him worthy, he kept his feelings to himself. It so happened that Sir Charles Trevor came to suspect Maurice's love for his fiancée and this, coupled with his envy of Fortescue's good looks, universal popularity and sunny disposition, caused resentment to burn within him. He decided to cause his adversary as much grief as possible. He would marry Alice very soon and then make sure that he flaunted her before Fortescue. One day as he was approaching Tiverton Castle, the dastardly Sir Charles pictured the hurt his wedding would cause his rival and, letting out a whoop of joy, he hurled his hat into the air in jubilation. At that moment Maurice's faithful hound Vulcan bounded from the castle. It seized the hat and playfully shook it to pieces. Enraged, Sir Charles drew his sword and slew the dog on the spot. Maurice (who had been following a little way behind) let out a howl of indignation, rushed up to Sir Charles, and floored him with a well-aimed punch. The slighted fiancé demanded satisfaction, and told Fortescue to meet him in the woods near the river at seven o'clock that evening.

Maurice was no coward, but he knew that Sir Charles Trevor was a renowned swordsman against whose skills his

and terrifying darkness. The second ghost to wander this magnificent castle is that of the 'Grey Lady'. This sombre revenant has been seen many times, either enjoying a nebulous stroll between the castle and Powderham Church, or flitting about the library where she leaves a cold chill in her spectral wake. She is thought to be Lady Frances, who married Viscount Courtenay in 1741, and her appearances are said to be an ill omen that presage the death of the head of the family.

TIVERTON CASTLE
Tiverton, Devon Ⓐ Ⓣ 🛏
LOVERS' REPRIEVE

Built in 1106 by Richard de Redvers, whose family were the first Earls of Devon, Tiverton Castle was enlarged by their successors the Courtenays, who regarded it as their 'head and chief mansion'. The Courtenays remained here for some 260

ABOVE: Taunton Castle was the scene of a hearty celebration that came to a bloody end – and the sounds of ghostly merriment can still be heard.

OPPOSITE: Tiverton Castle was built in the early years of the 12th century, but the joyful ghosts of two wronged lovers, united in death, still roam in the woods.

limited abilities would be no match in a duel. Realizing his days were numbered, Maurice went to bid Alice farewell, and told her of his secret love for her. She burst into tears and told him that she felt the same way towards him. As Maurice left, she swore that if he were killed, her heart would die with him.

At the appointed time Sir Charles Trevor and Maurice Fortescue faced each other on the wooded banks of the rain-swelled River Exe. Moments later, the clash of steel echoed through the trees as the two men fought for their honour and their lives. Maurice succeeded in drawing the first blood, inflicting a wound on his rival's arm; but moments later he was dead, Sir Charles's sword protruding from his neck. Laughing triumphantly, the victor placed a contemptuous boot on his adversary's throat and, having removed his sword, kicked the lifeless body into the river. Suddenly a cry of despair sounded from the direction of the castle. Alice, who had been watching the duel from the walls, ran to the river and followed her lover

into its raging waters. Ever since, when the Exe is in flood, the couple's ghosts, closely followed by the faithful Vulcan, are said to walk together in the woods beneath the castle. Alice and Maurice walk arm in arm, chatting happily, delighted to have found in death the unity that was denied them in life.

TAUNTON CASTLE
Taunton, Somerset Ⓐ 🛏
A NEVER-ENDING PARTY

Taunton Castle was built in the 12th century and stands on the site of a Saxon earthwork fortification. Although it has, doubtless, witnessed much happiness and considerably more tragedy, one particular event has left an indelible stain upon its fabric and caused several ghosts to roam through what is now part hotel and part museum.

James Scott, 1st Duke of Monmouth (1649–85) was the illegitimate son of King Charles II and his mistress Lucy Walter. Determined to win the throne from his uncle, James II, the duke returned to England from Holland, and landed at Lyme Regis, Dorset, on 11th June 1685. He and his followers captured Taunton and took up residence in the castle, and the Duke was proclaimed king. That night his supporters celebrated at the castle, quaffing large quantities of wine and

dancing with ladies who were loyal to his cause. But their high spirits were short-lived. In the early hours of the morning of 6th July 1685, Monmouth's army suffered a crushing defeat at the Battle of Sedgemoor. On 15th July, the Duke of Monmouth was beheaded in London. His uncle, the king, sent the infamous Judge Jeffreys to the West Country to mete out savage retribution at the notorious 'Bloody Assizes'.

It was in the Great Hall of the castle that the Taunton Assize was held, and here 'Hanging Judge Jeffreys' condemned 200 of the duke's followers to the gallows, while many more were sold into slavery. The women, who had so recently danced in celebration in that very hall, were sentenced to be flogged.

Needless to say, the strong emotions of those long-ago events still linger at Taunton Castle. The museum that occupies the Great Hall often echoes to the steady tramp of invisible boots, as unseen soldiers drag the hapless followers of the ill-fated duke before the diabolical Jeffreys. Meanwhile at the Castle Hotel, guests often hear the ghostly, though soothing, strains of a phantom fiddle, said to be the ethereal tones of the duke and his followers as they continue to celebrate the victory that they were so certain would soon be theirs.

DUNSTER CASTLE
Dunster, Somerset Ⓐ 🌳
IN THE FIRING LINE

Rising from its sylvan cradle, the dramatic towers and majestic gables of Dunster Castle present as picturesque a stronghold as you could wish to encounter. William de Mohun built the original castle on a site granted him by William the Conqueror. His most infamous descendant was the third William de Mohun, a fanatical supporter of the Empress Matilda in her Civil War against King Stephen. De Mohun was known as the 'Scourge of the West' on account of his frequent bouts of plunder and burning in the locality. When Stephen besieged the stronghold, de Mohun set about minting his own coinage there, an action that may be responsible for the ghostly chinking of money that is often heard about the castle, especially on the nights of a full moon.

The direct male line of the family died out in 1376, and ownership of the castle passed to Lady Elizabeth Luttrell, whose descendants held it for six centuries. It was probably they who built the imposing gatehouse, which dates from around 1400 and is now the oldest part of Dunster Castle.

Although the Luttrells were not Royalists, the castle was seized in the Civil War and held by a Royalist garrison. Besieged by the Parliamentarians, who battered the castle walls with their heavy artillery, the governor Colonel Wyndham

OPPOSITE: When thunderclouds gather around Dunster Castle, an elderly, but proud female figure from the 17th century glides among the corridors and castle precincts.

held out for 160 days. At one point, legend claims, the Roundhead commander, Colonel Blake, threatened to stand Wyndham's mother in the line of fire unless he surrendered. However, when the spirited old lady gallantly urged her son to do his duty, Blake reconsidered and backed down. In April 1646, with the Royalist strongholds everywhere hauling down their flags in despair at the collapse of their cause, Wyndham finally surrendered the castle.

Every so often, the proud figure of an elderly woman, garbed in 17th-century dress, has been seen flitting around the corridors and precincts of the castle. She is a silent and harmless spectre whose favoured time of walking is whenever the air is heavy with thunder.

By the 19th century, the Luttrell family was intent on making the castle more comely than commanding, and employed Anthony Salvin who carried out considerable remodelling. The result is the delightful castle that is now owned by the National Trust and where, in addition to the aforementioned hauntings, a ghostly Roundhead makes occasional returns to the gatehouse's spectacular Leather Room, where his habit of disappearing into a closed and solid door both amazes and astonishes visitors.

FARLEIGH HUNGERFORD CASTLE
Farleigh, Somerset Ⓐ Ⓔ
THE DEADLY LADY HUNGERFORD

In 1369, the immensely wealthy Sir Thomas Hungerford, John of Gaunt's steward and first Speaker of the House of Commons, purchased the manor of Farleigh and set about rebuilding and enlarging the castle. Almost immediately he found himself in trouble, when he was charged with crenellating without a licence. However, he obtained a pardon in 1383, and was able to pass on a substantial stronghold to his son, Walter. Walter further enhanced the family seat and was created Baron Hungerford in 1426, and thenceforward the building became known as Farleigh Hungerford Castle.

Walter fought alongside Henry V at Agincourt. His grandson, Robert, although inheriting Walter's fighting genes, lacked his grandfather's ability to back the right side. He was captured in the last battle of the Hundred Years War, and spent seven years as a prisoner in France. Returning to England, he joined the Lancastrian cause in the Wars of the Roses and, on 29th March 1641, following the virtual annihilation of Henry VI's army at the Battle of Towton, was captured and executed. Farleigh Hungerford Castle then passed into the hands of Richard, Duke of Gloucester, later Richard III, who retained it until his defeat at Bosworth Field. The new king, Henry VII, returned Farleigh to Robert's grandson, Walter Hungerford. In 1516, Walter's son Edward inherited the estate and married Agnes, the widow of John Cotell. Following Edward's death in 1522, Lady Agnes Hungerford was arrested on suspicion of murdering her first husband. It was alleged that she had had him strangled and his body burnt in the kitchen furnace at Farleigh Hungerford. Found guilty, she was hanged at London's Tyburn.

Her stepson, another Walter, was married three times. Nothing is known of his first two wives, but his third spouse created a sensation when she wrote to Thomas Cromwell complaining that her husband had imprisoned her in a castle tower for the previous three years and had even tried to poison her. Walter and Cromwell were friends, however, and the latter ignored Lady Hungerford's plight. In 1540, Thomas Cromwell fell from royal favour and, shortly afterwards, Walter was executed on charges of treason and 'unnatural vices'. Lady Hungerford emerged from her captivity and married Sir Robert Throckmorton, by whom she had six children.

Farleigh Hungerford Castle passed to the Crown and was then sold back to Walter's son Edward, who kept alive the family's tradition of intrigue by accusing his wife of trying to poison him. The case was dismissed in court, and Edward, having refused to pay his wife's legal costs, was sent to prison for debt. However, the curtain was fast descending upon the almost Shakespearean plot that is the history of this remarkable clan. In the latter half of the 17th century, another Sir Edward, whom posterity remembers as 'the Hungerford waster', inherited the estate and proceeded to gamble away the family fortune. He sold the castle in 1686, and thereafter it fell into ruin until only the bare ribs of the once magnificent pile remained.

The ghost of Lady Agnes Hungerford is still said to return here on occasion. She appears in the vicinity of the chapel, a serenely beautiful shade who flickers briefly in front of astonished witnesses before fading into nothingness in those twilight moments when day turns to night.

OPPOSITE: Ruined walls tower above where the kitchens of Farleigh Hungerford Castle once were, and where, in the massive ovens, a 16th-century wife could conveniently dispose of her husband.

BELOW: Parts of Farleigh Hungerford Castle look civilized enough today, but former residents showed a dreadful propensity for attempting to harm one another.

PHANTOM FORTRESSES where GREY LADIES WATCH

My phantom-footed shape will go
When nightfall grays
Hither and thither along the ways
I and another used to know
In backward days.

FROM *MY SPIRIT WILL NOT HAUNT THE MOUND*
BY THOMAS HARDY (1840–1928)

DORSET, WILTSHIRE & HAMPSHIRE

The mark of history hangs heavy over the mysterious hillsides and ancient towns of this legendary landscape. It once formed the core of the Saxon Kingdom of Wessex and it was here, under the inspired leadership of Alfred the Great, that the united English nation was forged. Later, the Normans would build mighty castles here, in several cases utilizing the fortifications of earlier Roman strongholds that had been built against the threat posed by marauding Saxons. Long before this time a forgotten people had already wandered down the dusty byways to leave their mark upon the countryside. They carved mysterious figures into the chalk hillsides, and threw up huge earthworks of remarkable and breath-taking proportions. They also built impressive temples, such as those at Avebury and Stonehenge, which still strike wonder in even the most jaded among us. Imposing as the castles that litter the region are, they often pale in significance in comparison to these places of ancient mystery where man has worshipped for thousands of years.

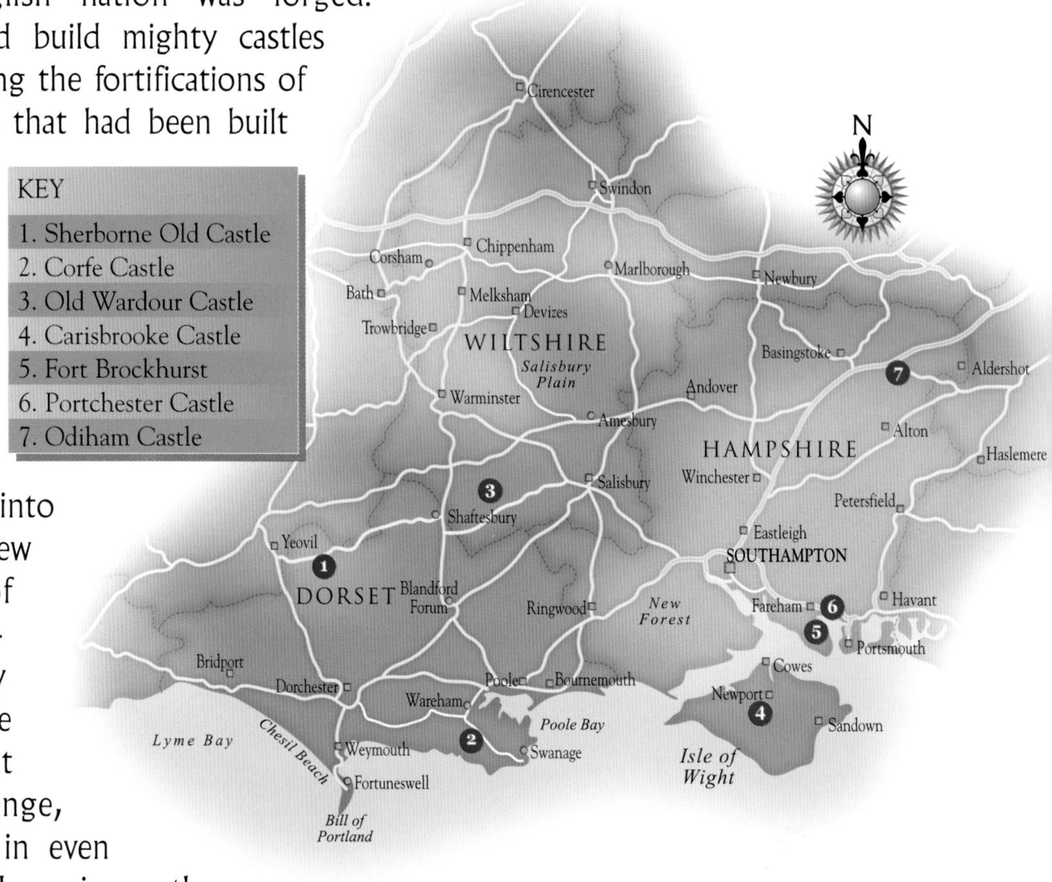

KEY
1. Sherborne Old Castle
2. Corfe Castle
3. Old Wardour Castle
4. Carisbrooke Castle
5. Fort Brockhurst
6. Portchester Castle
7. Odiham Castle

SHERBORNE OLD CASTLE
Sherborne, Dorset Ⓐ Ⓔ
THE BISHOP'S CURSE AND THE HERO

In the reign of Elizabeth I, Sir Walter Ralegh (1552–1618) was en route from London to Plymouth when he spied the soaring walls of Sherborne Castle and, literally, fell head over heels in love with it. According to Sir John Harrington in his *Nugae*

Antiquae, as Sir Walter was exploring the castle grounds his horse stumbled, and Ralegh's 'very face, which was then thought a very good face, ploughed up the earth where he fell'.

The castle had been built in the 12th century by one of the great fighting bishops of the age, Roger of Sarum. By Ralegh's time, it was still owned by his successors in the See of Salisbury. Unperturbed by a curse placed on the property by St Osmund, a former Bishop of Salisbury, that threatened destruction to anyone who removed the castle from ecclesiastical hands, Sir Walter began dropping hints to the queen that she might like to reward his services with the gift of his dream home. His persistence paid off, and in January 1592 he was awarded with a 99-year lease on Sherborne Castle.

Almost immediately, the dark shadow of St Osmund's curse fell upon him. Unbeknown to the queen, Sir Walter had secretly married Elizabeth Throckmorton, one of her cherished and jealously guarded maids of honour. On 29th March 1592, Bess gave birth to a son, and shortly afterwards, court gossip brought their indiscretion to the queen's attention. Having incurred the infamous royal wrath, the proud parents were soon languishing in the Tower of London, where Ralegh attempted suicide. He was saved only by the timely intervention of an official who wrenched the dagger from his grip.

Ralegh and Bess were finally released just before Christmas, 1592. They returned to Sherborne where, now in disgrace, Ralegh began embellishing their rural retreat. The cost of modernizing the old castle proved exorbitant, so the family abandoned it and built a suitably impressive home in Sherborne's old deer park. It was here, as he enjoyed a pipe of tobacco beneath the spreading branches of a great oak, that one of Ralegh's servants is said to have doused his master with a pitcher of beer in the mistaken belief that his beard was on fire.

Although Ralegh would later win his way back into Elizabeth I's favour, the curse struck again when her successor, James I, ascended the throne. In July 1603, Ralegh was implicated in a plot instigated by Lord Cobham, to replace James with his cousin, Lady Arabella Stewart. Shortly afterwards, Ralegh was again confined to the Tower of London, charged with high treason. He was sentenced to death, and although his life was spared, remained imprisoned for the next 13 years. His estate was given to James's favourite, Robert Carr, Earl of Somerset.

St Osmund's curse soon blighted the new owner of Sherborne Castle. Robert Carr had fallen in love with Frances Howard, child bride of Robert Devereux, Earl of Essex. Wishing to save herself for Carr, Frances consulted a quack astrologer who provided drugs that would render her husband impotent. For three years, the unfortunate Devereux struggled to consummate his marriage, before his inability to do so led to divorce. In 1613, following the king's intervention, Frances Howard was free to marry Robert Carr. Carr's mentor, Sir Thomas Overbury, made no secret of his dislike for Frances and her ambitious family, and urged his protégé to reconsider. He had, however, underestimated the influence that Frances and, more particularly her uncle, Henry Howard, wielded at court. Following another intervention by James I, Sir Thomas was sent to the Tower. Here, Frances Howard, assisted by Gervase Elwys, a compliant gaoler, began supplying Overbury with delectable

ABOVE: The late afternoon sun casts long shadows among the ruins of Sherborne Old Castle, where the ghost of Sir Walter Ralegh still walks a time-worn path.

PREVIOUS PAGES: The decayed outlines of Odiham Castle, neglected among unkempt woodland, belie the fact that this was once a favourite castle of King John of England.

tarts, all laced with poison. Sir Thomas died in excruciating pain. The Howards managed to keep secret their involvement in Sir Thomas' death for almost a year until, faced with escalating rumours, Elwys the gaoler panicked and confessed. The subsequent scandal severely discredited the court of James I. He quickly withdrew his favouritism from Robert Carr, who not only lost Sherborne Castle, but also — as if reiterating the power of St Osmund's curse — found himself incarcerated in Ralegh's newly vacated apartments at the Tower of London. Fortunately for him, his social standing and previous place in James's affections meant that

'WHAT DoST THoU FEAR? STRIKE, MAN, STRIKE!'

SIR WALTER RALEGH TO HIS EXECUTIONER

he was spared execution. Ralegh had been released just a week earlier, having persuaded the King to send him on a voyage to bring back treasure from Guiana. After almost a year of preparation, Ralegh set sail in 1617. The escapade was a disaster, marred by illness and crew mutinies. It ended in a catastrophic clash with the Spanish, during which Ralegh's own son, Walter, was killed when he disobeyed the king's orders and led a charge against the citadel at St Thôme. On his return Ralegh was once more imprisoned in the Tower of London, from where he was taken for trial and, on 28th October 1618, he learned that he was to be beheaded the next morning.

Ralegh went to his death bravely. As he stood on the scaffold he asked to see the axe and, running his finger along its blade, pronounced it 'a sharp medicine, but a sure cure for all diseases'. As he knelt at the block, someone asked if he would prefer to face east, looking towards the Promised Land. 'So the heart be right,' he replied 'it is no matter which way the head lieth.' He refused a blindfold, observing stoically, 'Think you I fear the shadow of the axe when I fear not the axe itself?' Having prayed for a minute, Ralegh gave the signal for the axe to fall. But the executioner was unable to move. Again the signal was given, but still the axeman remained motionless. 'What dost thou fear?' cried Ralegh. 'Strike, man, strike!'

At this the executioner finally struck, but took two blows to remove Ralegh's head. Holding it aloft, the executioner attempted to pronounce the traditional denunciation, 'Behold the head of a traitor'. But the words wouldn't come, and it was left to an anonymous voice from the crowd to express the sentiments of most present, 'We have not another such head to be cut off!'

By this time, the Sherborne estate had been sold to Sir John Digby (1580–1653), whose descendants still own it. During the Civil War, the 12th-century castle was reduced to a ruin, and the nearby lodge, built by Ralegh in 1594, assumed the title of Sherborne Castle. Today, the crumbling walls of Sherborne Old Castle provide a sharp contrast to the stately grandeur of what is now the family home of the Wingfield Digbys. It is to the grounds hereabouts that the proud spirit of Sir Walter Ralegh makes an annual pilgrimage on St Michael's Eve (29th September), to roam once more the place where he spent some of his happiest and most settled years.

CORFE CASTLE
Wareham, Dorset Ⓐ 🌿
WHITE ROYAL LADY

Impressively situated on its lofty throne and protected by steep cliffs, this once vast fortress is now little more than a hollow shell. Having crossed the stone bridge that spans its deep moat, you find yourself wandering amid stark, monolithic columns or meandering through narrow corridors where ancient walls lean towards you at strange, almost threatening angles. William the Conqueror began building the castle,

BELOW: Wandering among the ragged remnants of Corfe Castle can be a spine-chilling experience if its resident 'white lady' honours you with a visit.

although it was King John who turned it into the royal palace, the melancholic ruins of which survive today. During the English Civil War, the redoubtable supporter of the king, Lady Bankes defended it until she was betrayed. One of her own garrison allowed Parliamentary soldiers to gain possession of the building, whereupon they set about destroying it. They toppled its mighty walls and undermined its foundations until – within a short period of time – nothing but the bare ribs of the once regal pile remained.

An aura of mystery soon descended as people began to whisper of ghostly encounters amid the mouldering ruins. Strange, flickering lights were seen moving about the ramparts at night. The heart-rending sobs of a weeping child were heard in a cottage that abuts the rocky knoll on which the castle stands. The most persistent of all the spectres, however, is the headless White Lady, whose shimmering shade chills the blood of those who chance upon

ABOVE: Visit the stairwells of Old Wardour Castle at twilight for a chance to see the phantom of Lady Blanche Arundell, who bravely defended against the Parliamentarians.

BELOW: Old Wardour is a classic four-towered, 14th-century castle, but its principle ghosts hail from the 1600s.

her, causing them to shiver and shake until she turns and drifts slowly away, fading into nothingness.

OLD WARDOUR CASTLE
Nr Shaftesbury, Wiltshire Ⓐ Ⓔ
THE HARBINGERS OF DEATH

In May 1643, a Parliamentary force of around 1,300 soldiers laid siege to Old Wardour Castle. It was defended only by Lady Blanche Arundell and 25 of her faithful retainers. The attackers, no doubt expected a quick victory. They had, however, misjudged the determined Lady Blanche, for she managed to hold out for five days and only surrendered after two mines had been exploded under the walls. The Parliamentarians then garrisoned Wardour, but the following year, after the death of Lord Arundell, his successor returned with a small force. After a four-month siege, they took back the fortress that had been built by Arundell's ancestors in the 14th century. The damage sustained as a result of the sieges was so great that the family had to live in the corn store. The castle was never repaired. The family died out in the 20th century, and it is therefore

unlikely that one of castle's more unique supernatural phenomena will ever be repeated. It was always said that whenever the death of a family member was close at hand, white owls would flutter around the castle to warn of the approaching tragedy. Although prophetic owls may be a thing of the past, the intrepid ghost hunter who ventures to this unusual, though romantic ruin, may be amply rewarded with a manifestation of Lady Blanche. As twilight creeps through the nooks and crannies of her old home, where she once loaded the matchlock guns for her faithful companions, she appears in doleful contemplation upon the walls.

CARISBROOKE CASTLE
Nr Newport, Isle of Wight Ⓐ Ⓔ
THE HAUNTED MOAT

William FitzOsberne began building the Norman castle at Carisbrooke on the site of a Roman fort that had become a Saxon stronghold. In 1078, the castle was forfeited to the Crown, and in 1100 granted to the de Redvers family, who built most of the imposing fortress that is visible today. The impressive twin-towered gatehouse was built in the 14th century, and Elizabethan defences were added later.

In 1647, Charles I became a prisoner at Carisbrooke Castle. His liberties were restricted to recreational walks along the walls and games of bowls on the old barbican outside the castle, which was specially converted for the purpose. Meanwhile, the king's friends were making efforts to enable his escape. The first attempt failed because the king could not force himself between the iron bars of his window. A second attempt was planned for 28th May 1648 when the king, having acquired nitric acid, endeavoured to cut through the bars and make a break for freedom. Unfortunately, the castle governor, a Colonel Hammond, learned of the plan and came to see the king, informing him: 'I am come to take leave of your majesty, for I hear you are going away...' Charles remained at Carisbrooke until September 1648 when he was moved to Newport, and then returned to London on 30th November. He was executed on 30th January 1649. After his death, his son, Prince Henry, and daughter Princess Elizabeth were sent to Carisbrooke Castle. Shortly after their arrival, the 14-year-old Elizabeth was found dead, her face resting on the Bible, which had been her father's last gift to her. It is with these tragic memories of the House of Stuart that the history of Carisbrooke closes. For although it is still the residence of the Governor of the Isle of Wight, no other events of such historical importance have occurred there.

The moat appears to be one of the most haunted parts of the castle and a 'Grey Lady' and a 'huge man in a long white gown' have been seen here. One female visitor strolling around the moat was even approached by a young man in a leather jerkin, who talked to her for several minutes and then, rather rudely, disappeared without finishing the conversation.

FORT BROCKHURST
Nr Gosport, Hampshire Ⓐ Ⓔ
THE WHISTLING SERGEANT MAJOR

Although one of five forts built between 1858–62 to protect Portsmouth Harbour and naval installations on the Gosport peninsula, Fort Brockhurst has the atmosphere of a medieval castle, right down to its drawbridge entrance which spans a water-filled moat. The

ABOVE: Charles I, the only English monarch to have been executed.

LEFT: Grim Carisbrooke Castle greeted Charles I, when he was taken there as prisoner in 1647. After his execution, his son and tragic daughter were also held there.

OPPOSITE: The dried-out and overgrown moat of Carisbrooke Castle is where you are likely to come across its anti-social spectre.

LEFT: The squat walls of the 19th-century Fort Brockhurst were designed to provide protection against artillery fire.

OPPOSITE: A long-dead lute player still occasionally plucks his melodious strings for the delectation of visitors to the crumbling Odiham Castle.

BELOW: Solid and resolute, the mighty walls of Portchester Castle have dominated the waters of Portsmouth Harbour for nigh on 2,000 years.

walls, however, are low and squat, since the high walls that made earlier strongholds so impregnable would have been easily destroyed by the new artillery of the 19th century. The interior is immense, and such is its spooky ambience that the London Vampyre Group chose it as the venue for their 'Gothic Feast of the Vampyres Banquet' in August 2002 (although the inclusion of a vegetarian option suggests a lack of commitment on the part of some members!).

A ghost that is more often heard than seen, and which appears to have a preference for cell number three, is said to haunt the fort. It is thought that the phantom footsteps that often echo through the corridors are those of a long-dead sergeant major making a spectral inspection of Fort Brockhurst. The measured tread of his footsteps is often accompanied by the sound of his tuneless whistling, as he repeats a ritual that he no doubt performed many times in his life and has continued for many years after his death.

PORTCHESTER CASTLE
Fareham, Hampshire Ⓐ Ⓔ
GHOSTLY MONKS AND DARK-HAIRED LADIES

Set against a spectacular backdrop and surrounded by the most complete Roman walls in northern Europe, the prodigious keep of Portchester Castle towers over the northern extremity of Portsmouth Harbour, a solid symbol of power with an eventful and chequered past.

Originally a Roman fort, it was constantly added to over the centuries and its impressive keep was probably raised in the 12th century. King John often stayed there and the ill-fated Edward II visited several times. Edward III used the castle as a

base while assembling his army that would sail for France and victory at Crécy. Following the peacemaking marriage of Richard II to Isabella, the seven-year-old daughter of the King of France, a royal palace in miniature was constructed within the old walls. Then, in 1415, Portchester Castle was the scene of another grand departure, as Henry V set off for his great victory at Agincourt. Thereafter the fortress declined in importance, and by the 18th century, its sole use was as a prison. It was filled to bursting during the Napoleonic Wars when 5,000 French prisoners were crammed into its solid bulk.

By May 1814, the prisoners were gone and the castle was allowed to fall into decay. Today the sheer magnitude of what remains is sufficient to set the imagination soaring into wild flights of historical fancy. This is aided by a number of past residents who occasionally return to the ruin in spirit form. The misty shade of 'something tall and whitish' is just one of the apparitions seen here. A ghostly monk who walks along the castle front, gradually disappearing as he goes, is another. Finally there is the melancholic dark-haired woman, whose fleeting phantom has been seen bending over a grave by the 12th-century church inside the castle grounds.

ODIHAM CASTLE
Odiham, Hampshire ®
THE SPECTRAL MAESTRO OF KING JOHN'S CASTLE

The few tattered remnants of Odiham Castle, nestling in quiet seclusion, are but a shadow of their former glory. Built between 1207 and 1212, it was reputedly one of King John's favourite castles and cost him about £10,000 to build. It was from here that the king set out to sign that fundamental statement of human liberties, the *Magna Carta*. Louis, Dauphin of France, captured the castle in 1216, after a 15-day siege. David of Scotland was later imprisoned there from 1346-47. Although what is left bears little resemblance to the formidable bastion of old, every so often, a trapped memory seems to awaken from within to raise the hackles of those who wander among the ruins. It begins with a chill breeze that seems to emanate from the very walls. Then a faint murmur is heard, which crescendos into an ancient song, sung by some long-forgotten minstrel who entertains his invisible audience, accompanied by the soothing tones of a lute.

Battle-Scarred Borders *and* Tranquil Strongholds

There open fanes and gaping graves
Yawn level with the luminous waves;
But not the riches there that lie
In each idol's diamond eye –
Not the gaily-jewelled dead
Tempt the waters from their bed;
For no ripples curl, alas!
Along that wilderness of glass –
No swellings tell that winds may be
Upon some far-off happier sea –
No heavings hint that winds have been
On seas less hideously serene.

FROM *The City in the Sea*
by Edgar Allan Poe (1809–49)

HEREFORDSHIRE, GLOUCESTERSHIRE, WARWICKSHIRE, WEST MIDLANDS, WORCESTERSHIRE & OXFORDSHIRE

The counties that stretch from Oxfordshire to Herefordshire now possess a pastoral tranquillity that belies their battle-scarred and blood-drenched past. Indeed. so many momentous events of national importance have taken place here that the region has long been known as 'England's Cockpit'. Nowhere is this unsettled past more evident than in the castles that dot the landscape. The mighty bulk of Warwick Castle was once home to Richard Neville, Earl of Warwick, a man whom history now remembers simply as 'the Kingmaker'. The raddled walls of Goodrich Castle gaze forlornly at the border with Wales much as they have done since the 12th century when the castle was built to protect against the threat of a Welsh invasion. Then there is the stern façade of Berkeley Castle behind whose secretive walls Edward II met such an horrific end that its ramifications still echo down the centuries. Add to this the childhood home of that most tragic of figures, Lady Jane Grey, the so-called 'nine-day queen', and you have an eventful past from which the troubled shades often transcend the centuries to wander once more in the places where, in life, they experienced deep sadness or great happiness.

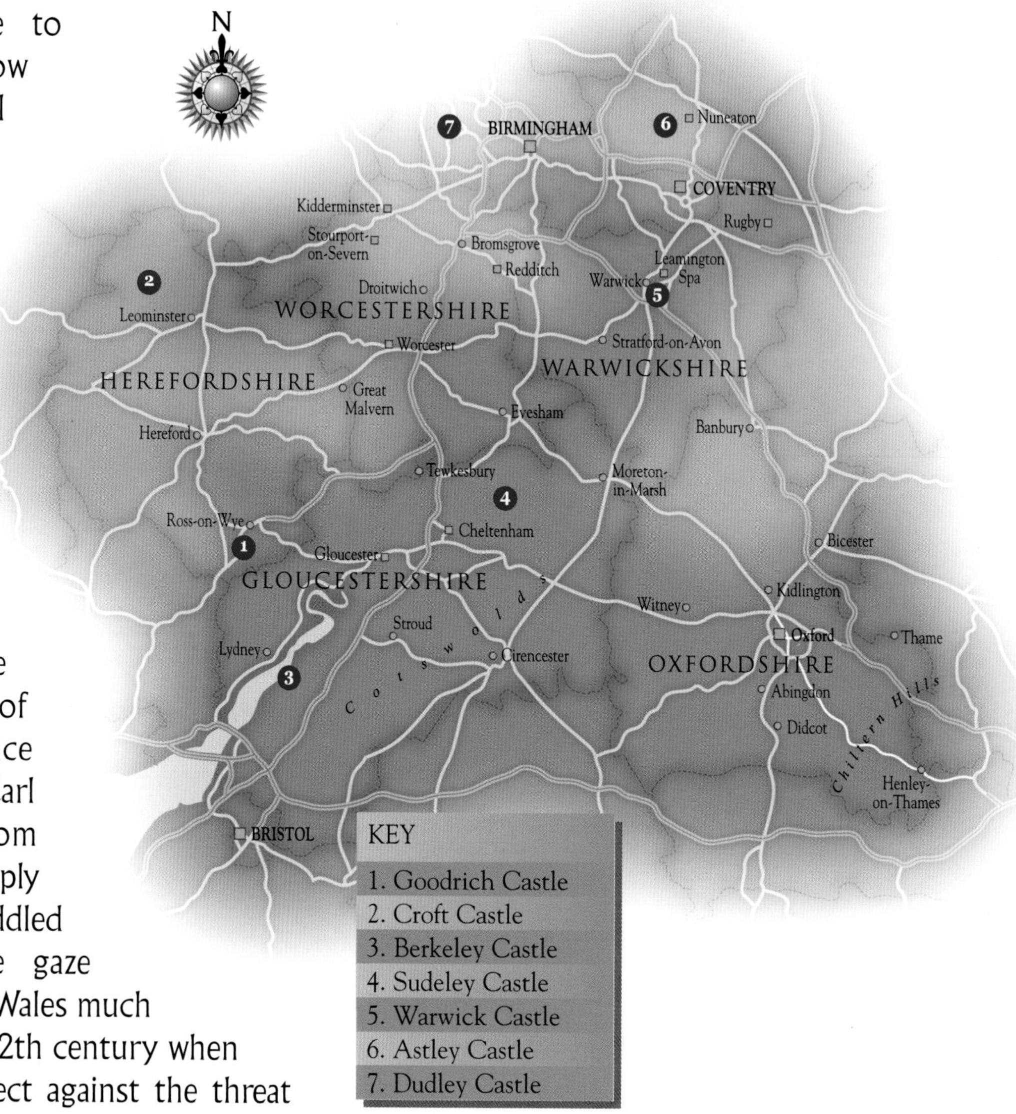

KEY

1. Goodrich Castle
2. Croft Castle
3. Berkeley Castle
4. Sudeley Castle
5. Warwick Castle
6. Astley Castle
7. Dudley Castle

GOODRICH CASTLE
Goodrich, Herefordshire Ⓐ Ⓔ
THE ETERNAL LOVERS AND THEIR WATERY FATE

ABOVE: The bedraggled wraiths of two 17th-century lovers have not managed to break their ties with Goodrich Castle.

PREVIOUS PAGES: Warwick Castle, the ultimate in medieval strongholds, was the site of a cruel murder in the 1600s.

The massive ruins of this red sandstone castle stand on a wooded, rocky spur overlooking the tranquil waters of the River Wye. They are pitted with numerous nooks and crannies that exude an aura of tragic mystery. The oldest part of the fortress is the grey stone keep, built in the 12th century when the castle was an important bastion on the border between England and Wales. Enlarged over succeeding centuries, it last saw action during the Civil War when it became a Royalist stronghold. Cromwell's troops attempted to breach its mighty walls by firing over 90kg (200lb) cannon balls at them from the aptly named mortar 'Roaring Meg'.

During the siege, Alice Birch, the niece of a Parliamentarian officer, took refuge in the castle with her Royalist lover, Charles Clifford. When it became apparent that the fortress would not be able to withstand the bombardment for much longer, Clifford and his young lover mounted his horse and, under cover of darkness, spurred the beast out of the castle and managed to break through the Roundhead ranks. Unfortunately, when they arrived at the muddy banks of the River Wye, they didn't realize that heavy rains had swollen its

waters. As they attempted to cross the raging torrent, their horse lost its footing and they were swept away to their deaths. Such was the trauma of their desperate bid for freedom that their bedraggled earthbound wraiths have been seen on stormy nights, urging a phantom horse into the wild waters of the Wye. On other occasions, passers-by late at night have seen their poignant spectres staring sadly from the ruined ramparts.

CROFT CASTLE
Nr Leominster, Herefordshire Ⓐ 🌿
THE GHOSTLY WELSH HERO

The avenues of magnificent trees that cradle Croft Castle in their protective embrace also lend it an air of secrecy. The de Croft family, for whom the castle is named, are thought to have arrived here from Normandy during the reign of Edward the Confessor. Having built their original fortress on the site they continued to embellish it over succeeding centuries. In the 14th century, Sir John de Croft married a daughter of the

Welsh nationalist Owain Glyndwr (1355–1416). In the 16th century, with the accession to the English throne of Henry VII, Sir Richard Croft became treasurer to the new monarch's household and, later, steward to his eldest son Prince Arthur. During the Civil War, the Crofts fought for Charles I and such was their loyalty that they allowed their stronghold to be dismantled to prevent its falling into Parliamentarian hands. In the mid-18th century, family debt forced them to sell the castle to Richard Knight of Downton, although the family reacquired it in 1923. Although the National Trust now runs it, members of the family still live here and ghosts from its illustrious past still wander the sylvan grounds and stunning interior.

Most famous is a giant of a man, clad in leather, said to be the ghost of Owain Glyndwr. His Grace, the Archbishop of Sydney, saw him in the early 20th century. There are those who would deny that it is possible for Glyndwr's ghost to haunt the castle, since the place and date of his death remain one of history's great mysteries. He is a member of that select band of heroes who, it is claimed, never died but sleep at sundry secret locations, awaiting the day when their country needs them again.

ABOVE: No one knows for sure where the legendary Welsh freedom fighter, Owen Glyndwr, is buried, but his ghost is seen amid the sylvan setting of Croft Castle.

BELOW: The agonized screams of a long-ago act of infamy still echo from the night time shadows at Berkeley Castle.

BERKELEY CASTLE
Berkeley, Gloucestershire Ⓐ
THE DREADFUL DEATH OF EDWARD II

History has certainly left its mark upon this magnificent 12th-century monument in the heart of the picturesque Vale of Berkeley. Amazingly, it has remained in the possession of the same family for nigh on 800 action-packed years.

Visitors to the castle can still see a deep dungeon in the old keep, into which were once thrown the rotting carcasses of animals, accompanied every so often, it is said, by those of the lower classes who had offended the powerful Lord Berkeley. The stench rising from this disease-ridden, and malodorous pit must have been unbearable, but it also provided an exquisitely horrific way to punish those of noble birth who had incurred the wrath of the Berkeley family. A windowless and airless cell can be seen close by. Here, unfortunate nobles would be locked away, with only the stinking air from the nearby dungeon to breathe. It provided a convenient method by which to dispose of those who could not be seen to have been murdered, since few people could survive long in the dreadful and foetid atmosphere.

It was in this living hell that Edward II found himself confined in 1327, after he was deposed by his wife Queen Isabella and her lover Roger Mortimer. It was their intention that a few days in the dreadful chamber would bring about the king's death. But his constitution surprised them. He became ill, but recovered, and managed to survive five months in the loathsome cell. Clearly, a more direct approach was required and so the queen instructed Edward's gaolers, Sir John Maltravers and Sir Thomas Gurney, to dispose of her husband as they saw fit. And so, on 21st September 1327, Edward II suffered the most horrible death of any British monarch. The two men seized Edward and pinned him face down to the bed, whereupon ' a kind of horn or funnel was thrust into his fundament through which a red-hot spit was run up his bowels'. Such was the king's agony that his screams are said to have been heard far beyond the castle walls and have echoed down the centuries on the anniversary of his death ever since.

ABOVE: King Edward 11, betrayed and deposed by his own wife, suffered one of the most horrific ends ever suffered by a king of England at Berkeley Castle.

SUDELEY CASTLE
Nr Winchcombe, Gloucestershire Ⓐ
MUCH WIT AND LITTLE JUDGEMENT

In 1441, Ralph Boteler, having been created Baron Sudeley and Lord Chamberlain of the King's Household, set about building a castle that would reflect his new status. Twenty years later, the new king, Edward IV cast covetous eyes upon the magnificent pile. He had the Lancastrian Boteler arrested on trumped up charges of treason, and confiscated his grand home. 'Sudeley Castle, thou art the traitor, not I,' Boteler is reputed to have observed as he was led away.

The castle was given to the king's brother, the Duke of Gloucester, later the infamous Richard III and, following his death at the Battle of Bosworth in 1485, was awarded to Jasper Tudor, the uncle of the new king, Henry VII. In 1537, Jane Seymour bore Henry VIII his longed-for son, Edward and the king showed his gratitude by creating her younger brother, Thomas, Lord Seymour of Sudeley.

The unfortunate Jane, however, died shortly after giving birth. Henry VIII would marry a further three times, his last wife being Catherine Parr, who had already been courted by Thomas Seymour. Following Henry's death in 1547, Seymour proposed marriage to the 15-year-old Princess Elizabeth, the king's daughter by Anne Boleyn. She turned him down, but ever the ambitious pragmatist, he rekindled his affair with her stepmother. Less than a month after being widowed, Catherine Parr had accepted Seymour's marriage proposal.

The newly-weds moved into Sudeley Castle, where on 30th August 1548, Catherine gave birth to a daughter, Mary. The couple were overjoyed. But a week later, Catherine died of puerperal fever and was buried in the castle's chapel of St Mary. She was not to rest peacefully. After the Civil War over a century later, her grave lay neglected. In 1782, a farmer discovered it and, opening the lead casket, found the body intact and uncorrupted. Moments later, the cadaver crumbled into dust, and the terrified man hastily reburied the queen. She was finally reinterred in the new chapel in 1817, and there she now lies beneath a splendid Victorian effigy. Her daughter, Mary, simply disappeared from the pages of history, and her fate is unknown.

Catherine's ghost is still said to wander the cosy corridors of Sudeley Castle, and there have been frequent reports of a tall lady in a green dress seen around the castle nursery. Her appearances are often presaged by the faint smell of apple-scented perfume, and occasionally accompanied by the heart-rending sobs of a crying child.

Lord Thomas Seymour of Sudely refused to allow widowhood to stand in the way of his ambitions. He renewed his wooing of Princess Elizabeth, and when she rebuffed him, made similar assignations to her half-sister, Mary (Mary Tudor, daughter of Catherine of Aragon). Having no success with either princess, he attempted instead to gain the confidence of the boy-king, the staunchly Protestant Edward VI. One of the main obstacles to Thomas's ambition was that his own brother, Edward, held the influential position of Protector of the Realm and was monopolizing access to the monarch. Thomas attempted to turn the young king against his protector. But this lust for power proved to be Thomas Seymour's downfall. He was arrested on charges of treason,

'THIS DAY DIED A MAN OF MUCH WIT, AND VERY LITTLE JUDGEMENT.'

PRINCESS ELIZABETH ON THE DEATH OF THOMAS SEYMOUR

found guilty and executed. His death warrant was signed by his own brother, the Lord Protector. When Princess Elizabeth learnt of Thomas Seymour's death, she wrote: 'This day died a man of much wit, and very little judgement'.

Sudeley Castle passed to the Duke of Northumberland, who persuaded the dying Edward VI to name Lady Jane Grey as his successor to keep the throne Protestant. But opinion was against Lady Jane; she was queen for less than a fortnight before being succeeded by Mary Tudor. Northumberland's lands were confiscated, and several months after her brief reign, Jane Grey was executed. Sudeley's days of glory were over, and after the Civil War it gradually fell into ruin.

In the 19th century, Sudeley Castle was restored to its former glory, and today is the home of Lord and Lady Ashcombe and the Dent-Brocklehurst family.

Another restless wraith that haunts Sudeley is that of a 19th-century house-keeper whose name was Janet. This formidable Scottish lady took the virtues of her young housemaids very seriously, and each night would sit at the top of the stairs leading to their sleeping quarters, armed with a feather duster to fend off the amorous approaches of the young menservants. Death has, apparently, not loosed her grip on her domain, and several people ascending the stairs have reported encounters with her. A teenage girl, who one day strayed from her tour group, came face-to-face with the housekeeper on the upstairs landing. She became hysterical when the stern-faced apparition began waving her feather duster towards her in spectral rebuke.

WARWICK CASTLE
Warwick, Warwickshire Ⓐ
A GHOST IN THE STUDY

Sir Walter Scott called Warwick Castle 'the fairest monument of ancient chivalrous splendour which yet remained uninjured by time'. To pass through the castle's massive gatehouse and stand in the courtyard, gazing up at its lofty towers, is to feel that you've somehow slipped back in time. It would come as no surprise if a figure in burnished armour came striding towards you, hopefully in greeting! It is a solid and resolute bastion, an indefatigable symbol of power, whose history is indelibly linked to the history of England. It was here during the Wars of the Roses that 'the Kingmaker' Richard Neville, Earl of Warwick (1428–71) held the monarch he had 'made' – Edward IV – captive, while the king he had

ABOVE: Henry VI, whose weak and ineffectual reign was overshadowed by one of the most acute phases of the Wars of the Roses.

LEFT: A ghostly but moralistic housekeeper is just one of the many spirits to be seen at the 15th-century Sudeley Castle.

OPPOSITE: Warwick Castle has seen many deeds of treachery – including, maybe, Richard III's order for two young princes to be murdered.

removed – Henry VI – languished in the Tower of London. For a short time, Neville was the most powerful man in the land, and virtually ruled England until being cut down in his prime at the Battle of Barnet in 1471.

Later, Richard III spent time at Warwick. According to the great Tudor propagandist, Sir Thomas More, it was at Warwick Castle that the much-maligned monarch gave the order for the murder of the two Princes in the Tower (see page 46).

For those who come to this most castle-like of English castles seeking encounters of a more spine-tingling nature, the 'Ghost Tower' is the place to aim for. Sir Fulke Greville (1554–1628) was granted Warwick Castle by King James I in 1604. At the time, the place had been unoccupied for 14 years and was in a ruinous condition. Fortunately, Greville, as well as being a fine poet and playwright, was a rich and influential man who slowly converted Warwick Castle into 'the most princely seat within the midlands part of this realm'. Greville served as Chancellor of the Exchequer from 1614 to 1621. He was later raised to the peerage as Baron Brooke, and then made Commissioner of the Treasury.

Seven years later, thoughts of his own mortality led Greville to draw up a will. He had never married and had no children, so he decided to make slight provision for his servant, Ralph Haywood. Haywood was not impressed with the paltry bequest and, in a fit of rage, stabbed his master while helping him dress at his house in London. It took the unfortunate Greville a month to die, his agony compounded by the surgeon's insistence on packing the wound with mutton fat. He was brought back to Warwick Castle and his tomb can still be seen in nearby St Mary's Church. Greville's ghost returns to the castle to walk the room that was once his study. Here witnesses have reported catching fleeting glimpses of his sad shade staring at them from the dark corners, or feeling his presence at the place where he once composed such prophetic lines as:

If Nature did not take delight in blood,
She would have made more easy ways to good.

ASTLEY CASTLE
Astley, Nr Nuneton, Warwickshire Ⓡ
THE CHILDHOOD HAUNT

The fire-mangled ruins of this ancient castle sit alongside the tranquil churchyard of St Mary the Virgin in the sleepy Warwickshire village of Astley. It is a sad and neglected place whose pale red walls have collapsed, and whose moat has almost disappeared beneath an ocean of weed, nettle and bracken. A ring of massive trees shields it from prying eyes. There is nothing here to suggest that it was once the home of that most tragic of historic figures, Lady Jane Grey (1537–54), who reigned as Queen of England for only a period of days, and was later executed. Jane's father, Henry, Duke of Suffolk, came to Astley following the failure of his attempt to defeat Mary Tudor (who succeeded Jane as queen). Legend holds that he spent three days hiding in a tree in the churchyard, before being spotted by his grounds keeper who betrayed him. He was later beheaded, and his headless ghost has wandered Astley Castle ever since.

DUDLEY CASTLE
Dudley, West Midlands Ⓐ
THE GHOSTLY LEGS AND THE SOMBRE GREY LADY

Dudley Castle – the remnants of which stand atop a lofty, limestone crag, and which are reached via a stroll through Dudley Zoo – was founded in 1071. It was massively refortified in the 12th and 13th centuries by the owners, the de Somery

family who, tradition holds, resorted to violent extortion to fund the expansion. At least one member of this brutish clan may still reside amidst the shattered ruins.

In a dimly lit corner of the castle's lecture room are two halves of an enormous medieval stone coffin, the original occupant of which must have been a giant of his time. It came from Dudley Priory, where the Lords of Dudley were once buried, and is believed to have once held the mortal remains of John de Somery, who died in 1322. However, in 2002 an historical dowser detected that the two sections of the coffin, while both being from the 14th century, were of different dates and, therefore, may come from two different caskets. Such a discovery, of course, is merely academic, unless, that is, you happen to be one of the former incumbents, whose earthbound spirit has remained trapped at your place of interment. A cleaner, working in the room one day, happened to glance over in the direction of the coffin, and saw a pair of feet, clad in thigh-length riding boots, standing next to it. Her alarm intensified when she realized that the figure was minus the upper half of its body! Is it possible that the cleaving in two of his resting place has condemned John de Somery to lead a somewhat truncated ethereal existence?

From the de Somerys, the castle passed by marriage to the de Sutton family, and then in the mid-16th century, came into possession of John Dudley, Duke of Northumberland, who set about creating an abode that would match the lofty, and ultimately fatal, heights of his dynastic ambition. When Henry VIII died in 1547, John Dudley became a trusted confidant and adviser to Edward VI. Following the king's death in 1553, Dudley conspired to make his own daughter-in-law, Lady Jane Grey, Queen of England, thus by-passing the rightful heir, Mary Tudor. The plot floundered, as the country as a whole

OPPOSITE: Once the home of Lady Jane Grey, the fire-ravaged ruins of Astley Castle are now neglected.

ABOVE: The remnants of Dudley Castle command a rocky vantage point above the zoo that is there today.

supported Mary's claim. Dudley's fellow conspirators quickly deserted him, and the Duke was forced to surrender to the mercy of Mary I. This was not forthcoming and he, his son and the unfortunate nine-day queen, Lady Jane Grey, were all executed. The castle reverted to the Sutton family and thereafter sank into decline.

Dudley Castle was garrisoned by the Royalists during the Civil War and besieged by the Parliamentarians. Following the defeat of Charles I at the Battle of Naseby, it was surrendered on 13th May 1646, and the keep, gatehouse and portions of the curtain wall were subsequently slighted. Although the then owners, the Ward family, continued to use the domestic areas, they appear to have had little enthusiasm for the castle as a whole. On 24th July 1750, the castle was engulfed by fire and the flames were allowed to burn unabated for three days and nights. Dudley Castle settled into its role of romantic ruin until, in 1937, it was incorporated into the zoological gardens, above which it now looms.

Disembodied legs aside, many spirits linger around the lofty remnants. A group of intrepid ghost hunters who volunteered for a sponsored overnight stay one Hallowe'en were startled in the early hours by a mysterious figure, seen pacing across the parapets. Who, or what, it was has never been ascertained and it has never been seen since. The wraith of an old lady,

who hanged herself from the ramparts when her cat was killed by local youths, has also been known to return occasionally to the place of her suicide. A Civil War drummer, who was picked off by a single shot from the battlements as he attempted to take a message offering terms of surrender to the garrison, is also seen from time to time.

The most famous ghost is the Grey Lady, whose sombre shade drifts around the parapets of the old keep at all times of the day and night. She is thought to be Dorothy Beaumont, who died at the castle during the siege of 1646, apparently of natural causes. The Parliamentary commander, Sir William Brereton, allowed her funeral cortège to pass through his lines and she was buried in the church at the top of Dudley High Street. The fact that her infant child had died before her and been laid to rest in the town's lower church, closer to the castle, proved too much for Dorothy's spirit. Her ghost wanders the castle seeking the baby whom fate and the length of the High Street have separated her from for eternity. Staff are accustomed to her wanderings, and bemused visitors will testify to her existence. In the course of one of the ghost tours now staged at the castle, an actress was employed to play the part of Dorothy's ghost. At the crucial moment when the castle keeper, Adrian Durkin, was telling Dorothy's heart-rending tale, participants were puzzled when a second Grey Lady appeared behind the actress.

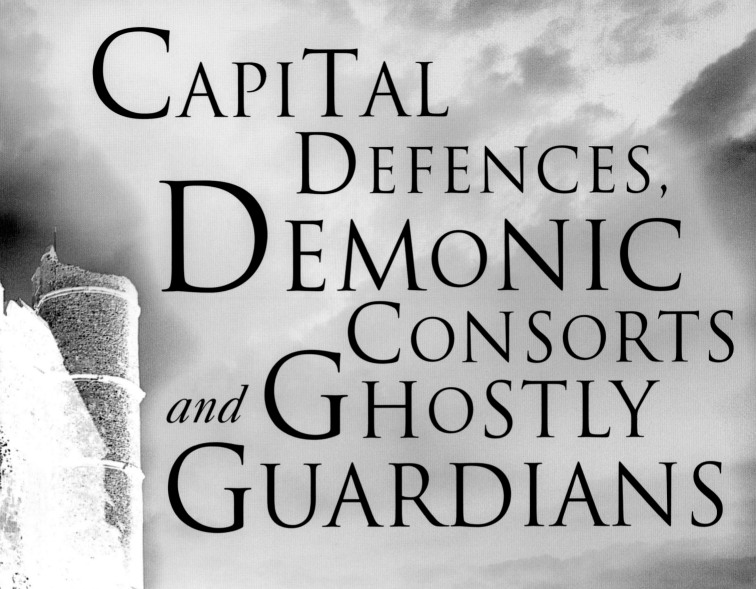

Capital Defences, Demonic Consorts and Ghostly Guardians

*I walk till the stars of London wane
And dawn creeps up the Shadwell Stair.
But when the crowing sirens blare
I with another ghost am lain.*

From Shadwell stair
by Wilfred Owen (1893–1918)

LONDON, BERKSHIRE, BUCKINGHAMSHIRE, BEDFORDSHIRE & HERTFORDSHIRE

London and the counties that stretch to its north and west possess a limited number of castles, few of which are haunted. Yet the intrepid seeker after things mysterious will find among the castles that are in the region some of the oldest inhabited and the most haunted in Britain. The Tower of London is a spectral township in its own right and the tales of the supernatural happenings that have occurred and continue to occur there merit a book of their own. The names of those who have passed through Traitors' Gate to be lost to the world thereafter read like a 'who's who' of English history, and the ghosts offer a veritable hierarchy of the spirit world. Windsor Castle, the Queen's favourite, is the largest and oldest inhabited castle in Europe, and has acquired a phantom population to match its lofty heights and venerable antiquity. So although this region might not possess as many castles as other parts of the country, it is certainly home to a greater concentration of castle ghosts. Just wandering around these two most magnificent strongholds, is to walk with some of the most illustrious — and infamous — names in the history of the British Isles.

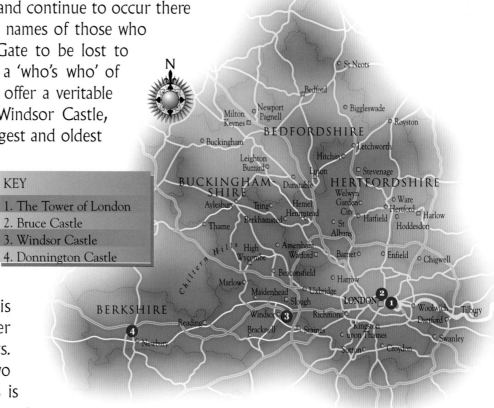

KEY

1. The Tower of London
2. Bruce Castle
3. Windsor Castle
4. Donnington Castle

THE TOWER OF LONDON
London Ⓐ
ENGLAND'S MOST HAUNTED BUILDING

Grim, grey and awe-inspiring, the Tower has dominated the London landscape and the capital's history since its construction by William the Conqueror in 1078. Today it is, perhaps, the most haunted building in England. The Wakefield Tower is haunted by the tragic English monarch, Henry VI, whose weak and ineffectual reign ended here with his murder 'in the hour before midnight' on 21st May 1471, as he knelt at prayer. Tradition asserts that the knife with which he was 'stikk'd full of deadly holes' was wielded by the Duke of Gloucester (later the infamous Richard III).

On the anniversary of his murder, Henry's mournful wraith is said to appear as the clock ticks towards midnight, and pace fitfully around the interior of the Wakefield Tower until, upon the last stroke of midnight, it fades slowly into the stone and rests peacefully for another year.

The massive White Tower is the oldest and most forbidding of all the Tower of London's buildings. Its winding stone corridors are the eerie haunt of a 'White Lady' who once stood at a window waving to a group of children in the building opposite. It may well be her 'cheap perfume' that impregnates the air around the entrance to St John's Chapel, and which has caused many a guard to retch upon inhaling its pungent aroma. In the gallery where Henry VIII's impressively enormous suit of armour is exhibited, several guards have spoken of a terrible crushing sensation that suddenly descends upon them as they enter, but which lifts the moment they stagger, shaking, from the room. A guard patrolling here

PREVIOUS PAGES: Ghosts from a long-ago siege may be among the shadowy occupants of the impressive Donnington Castle.

BELOW: The shadow of the executioner's axe falls over the Tower of London, one of England's most haunted sites.

one stormy night had the sudden and unnerving sensation that someone had thrown a heavy cloak over him. As he struggled to free himself, the garment was seized from behind and pulled tight around his throat. Managing to break free from its sinister grasp, he rushed back to the guardroom where the marks upon his neck bore vivid testimony to his brush with the phantom assailant.

A memorial on Tower Green remembers all those unfortunate souls who have been executed here over the centuries. Anne Boleyn and Lady Jane Grey are both said to return to the vicinity, whilst the ghost of Margaret Pole, Countess of Salisbury, roams here in a dramatic and alarming fashion. At the age of 72, she became an unwitting and undeserving target for Henry VIII's petty vengeance. Her son, Cardinal Pole, had vilified the king's claim as head of the Church in England. As the cardinal was safely ensconced in France, Henry had his mother brought to the block on 27th May 1541. The executioner told the spirited old lady to kneel, but she refused. 'So should traitors do and I am none,' she sneered. The executioner raised his axe, took a swing at her and then chased the screaming countess around the scaffold

where he, literally, hacked her to death. The shameful spectacle has been repeated several times on the anniversary of her death, as her shrieking phantom is pursued throughout eternity by a ghostly executioner.

The Bloody Tower, the very name of which conjures up all manner of gruesome images, is home to the most poignant shades that drift through this dreadful fortress. When Edward IV died suddenly in April 1483, his 12-year-old son was destined to succeed him as Edward V. However, before the boy's coronation could take place both he and his younger brother, Richard, had been declared illegitimate by Parliament. Their uncle, the Duke of Gloucester, duly ascended the throne as Richard III. The boys, meanwhile, had been sent to the Tower of London, ostensibly in preparation for Edward's coronation, and were often seen playing happily around the grounds. But around June 1483, they mysteriously vanished and were never seen alive again. It was always assumed that they had been murdered on Richard's instructions and their bodies buried somewhere within the grounds of the Tower. When two skeletons were uncovered beneath a staircase of the White Tower in 1674, they were presumed to be the remains of the two little princes and afforded royal burial in Westminster Abbey. The whimpering wraiths of the two children, dressed in white nightgowns and clutching each other in terror, have frequently been seen in the dimly lit rooms of their imprisonment. Witnesses are moved to pity and long to reach out and console the pathetic spectres. Should they do so, the trembling revenants back slowly against the wall and fade into the fabric.

Returning to the White Tower, and the fearless custody guards who wander its interior in the dead of night, there was the eerie occasion when one of them, a Mr Arthur Crick, decided to rest as he made his rounds. Sitting on a ledge, he slipped off a shoe and was in the process of massaging his foot, when a voice behind him whispered, 'There's only you and I here'. This elicited from Arthur the very earthly response, 'Just let me get this bloody shoe on and there'll only be you'!

ABOVE: The little princes, Edward and Richard, were murdered in one of the most infamous acts in the Tower of London's history.

BRUCE CASTLE
Tottenham, London Ⓐ
THE MELANCHOLIC SHADE OF LADY COLERAINE

Tradition holds that this Elizabethan manor house, once the home of postal reformer Sir Rowland Hill (1795–1879), stands on the site of a castle built by the father of King Robert the Bruce. The manor certainly did belong to the Scottish royal family at one time.

The window of a small chamber can be seen above the clock on the outside wall and it was here that Lord Coleraine is said to have imprisoned his beautiful wife, Constantia, together with their infant, for fear that anyone else should gaze upon her. Distraught at her detention, the poor lady was finally overcome by grief, and on 3rd November 1680 she took her baby in her arms, walked to the window and flung herself from the balustrade where mother and child crashed to their deaths on the paving stones below. Her disturbing screams continued to echo down the centuries and were heard each anniversary of her death. Then, in the early years of the 20th century a sympathetic clergyman took pity on her and held a prayer service in the room in the hope of laying her spirit to rest. Although he managed to quell the screams, her silent shade occasionally repeats her suicide, much to the consternation of astonished passers-by.

In July 1971, two people walking past the building late one night noticed a group of revellers in 18th-century costume, apparently enjoying a ball. What caught their attention was the fact that the guests were making no sound and appeared to be floating in mid air. Another couple saw the mysterious figures a few days later and this time were approaching them, when the revellers slowly melted into thin air.

'THERE'S ONLY YOU AND I HERE.'

OTHERWORLDLY VOICE TO A GUARD IN THE TOWER OF LONDON

WINDSOR CASTLE
Windsor, Berkshire Ⓐ
GHOSTLY QUEENS, TRAGIC KINGS AND FLEETING SHADOWS

Windsor Castle was originally one of the chain of castles flung up by William the Conqueror as he attempted to subjugate the vanquished Anglo-Saxons. Over the ensuing centuries, it was continually added to, and now has the distinction of being both the oldest and largest inhabited castle in Europe.

As you approach the castle you are greeted by an elegant statue of Queen Victoria, placed here in 1887 to commemorate her Golden Jubilee. It has long been rumoured that Victoria held several séances at the castle in an attempt to contact the spirit of her consort, Prince Albert, whose death in 1861 had left her bereft. It is also claimed that she used her faithful retainer, John Brown, as her medium and that she kept copious notes of these endeavours. These records were reputedly discovered after her death by the Dean of Windsor, who burnt them for fear that they might cause a royal scandal should their contents ever be made public.

In February 1897, Lieutenant Carr Glyn of the Grenadier Guards was sitting reading in the outer room of the queen's library, when a lady dressed in black walked past him, and turned a corner. Intrigued by the fact that she reminded him of the portraits he had seen of Elizabeth I, Glynn followed, but could find no trace of her. Furthermore, there was no doorway through which she could have left the library. He asked an attendant who the lady was, but was told that he was the only person who had entered the library that afternoon. The attendant then raised the possibility that the lieutenant had been honoured with a spectral sighting of Queen Elizabeth I.

Elizabeth I is not the only royal to undertake ghostly perambulations around the corridors and grounds of Windsor Castle, for apparitions of both Henry VIII and Charles I have also been seen here. It was just before Christmas 1648 that Charles Stuart was taken as a prisoner to Windsor Castle following the decision that he should be 'prosecuted for his life as a criminal person'. Following his trial and beheading in

ABOVE: Where the Elizabethan manor house known as Bruce Castle stands today may once have been the site of a castle built by the father of Scotland's Robert the Bruce.

London on 30th January 1649, his body was returned to Windsor to be buried in the same vault as Henry VIII and Jane Seymour. As the black-draped coffin was being carried towards

St George's Chapel, the sky, which until then had been 'serene and clear', clouded over and a sudden blizzard swept across the grounds. The black pall over the coffin was 'all white' by the time they reached the end of the chapel, and many took this as a divine sign proclaiming the king's innocence.

As a sick old man, George III spent much of his time at Windsor, and each day would take and return the afternoon salute of his guards. Following his death, while his body still lay in state, the guards were passing the king's window when the commanding officer saw the unmistakable figure of the king standing in his customary place. Instinctively he gave the order 'Eyes right', and as they swung round each soldier saw the figure and watched as he returned their salute.

In April 1906, a sentry was on duty one night at the top of the pathway beyond the main entrance to the castle when a group of men appeared from nowhere, and began walking towards him. Thinking they were intruders the sentry challenged them, but they continued to advance. When they ignored his third challenge, he cocked his rifle and fired at the leading figure, which paused momentarily but then continued forward. Raising his bayonet, the soldier charged at the group,

whereupon they promptly vanished into thin air. He reported the experience to his commanding officer and a full-scale search of the castle and grounds was undertaken, but no intruders were found and the sentry was confined to barracks for three days as punishment.

The view of the castle's south façade from the Long Walk in Windsor Great Park is stunning, although at night it can be sinister. It was here in 1927 that an 18-year-old guardsman, patrolling this area at night, was overcome with melancholy and shot himself. Some weeks later a colleague of his, Sergeant Leake, was given the same night duty. At the end of his shift, he was pleased to hear the footsteps of what he presumed to be his relief. Instead, he found himself gazing at the face of the young suicide. As he stood staring in astonishment, the genuine relief marched into view and the apparition vanished. Back at barracks, he reported his experience to several other sentries who all claimed to have witnessed manifestations of their dead associate.

Donnington Castle

Nr Newbury, Berkshire ® Ⓔ

THE CASTLE THAT WOULDN'T SURRENDER

Donnington Castle's towering gatehouse, standing on a high spur and overlooking the old London-to-Bath road, is an awesome edifice that commands attention much as it has done since its construction in 1386. Built by Richard de Abberbury, chamberlain to Richard II's queen, Anne of Bohemia, its most eventful period was during the Civil War when Charles I seized it from its owner, John Packer, and appointed John Boys commander of the garrison.

In July 1644, the Parliamentarian General Middleton arrived with 3,000 men and demanded that the garrison surrender. When Boys refused, Middleton launched an ill-conceived siege that not only failed to break through the castle's defences but also cost him a tenth of his force. In September, a new force under a new commander loosed a 12-day volley of cannon fire at the walls. Three of the castle's flanking towers were blown to smithereens and the curtain wall was breached, but still the valiant Boys refused to surrender. A month later, the Parliamentarians tried again and bombarded the castle with more than 1,000 shots. When they sent word demanding that Boys submit, they received short shrift. Then word arrived that Charles I was on his way to relieve the defenders and the attackers retreated. The exhausted garrison was reprovisioned and was able to enjoy a brief respite from hostilities.

When the second Battle of Newbury ended in stalemate on 28th October 1644, another assault on the castle led by Sir William Waller ensued. Once more, the demands for surrender were met with an emphatic 'no' from the gallant Boys, and a week later, a Royalist force commanded by Prince Rupert managed to relieve the garrison.

Colonel Boys used the respite afforded by the winter months to strengthen his defences and was once more prepared to continue his valiant stand. But the Civil War was drawing to a close. In March 1646, the Parliamentarians again demanded his surrender, so Boys sought the king's instructions and was told to get the best terms he could. On the 1st April 1646, having withstood almost 20 months of constant siege, John Boys surrendered to his adversaries. Parliament then voted for the demolition of the castle as it had become a symbol of valiant resistance. Today, all that remains are the twin towers of the mighty gatehouse, rising from the grassy hillside to a commanding 20 metres (65 feet).

Needless to say, such a turbulent history has resulted in several ghosts. There are persistent reports of a spectral white dog that comes bounding down the hill from the castle towards the woods below. The creature makes no sound, and the first intimation that he is anything other than living flesh and blood is when he suddenly vanishes into thin air. A ghostly guard has also been seen around the gatehouse. Whether he is the shade of one of the castle's Civil War defenders is unknown, since he never stays around long enough for witnesses to ask him! One minute he'll be standing by the gatehouse, a solid and apparently human figure, the next he will suddenly disappear, as one witness put it, 'like a bubble bursting'.

BELOW: The soaring bulk of Donnington Castle's gatehouse looms over its surroundings, while the thick walls crackle with the memories of past deeds.

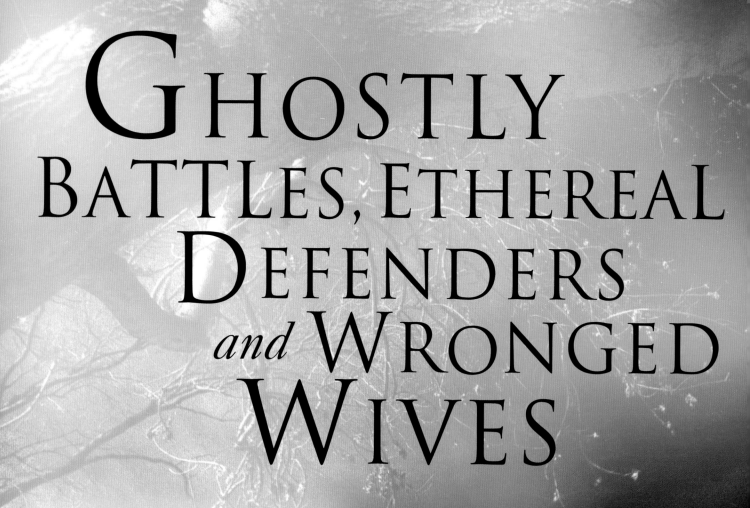

GHOSTLY BATTLES, ETHEREAL DEFENDERS *and* WRONGED WIVES

Soldier, rest! thy warfare o'er,
Sleep the sleep that knows not breaking;
Dream of battled fields no more,
Days of danger, nights of waking.
In our isle's enchanted hall,
Hands unseen thy couch are strewing,
Fairy strains of music fall,
Every sense in slumber dewing.

FROM *THE LADY OF THE LAKE*
BY SIR WALTER SCOTT (1771-1832)

does this disturbing phantom take on a recognizable guise. It assumes the shape of a stern-faced woman in a light-coloured gown, who fixes startled bystanders with a fearsome look of admonishment.

AMBERLEY CASTLE
Amberley, West Sussex
THE MELANCHOLIC VICTIM OF A LUSTFUL BISHOP

Amberley Castle is simply special. It stands as a proud reminder of the days when bishops were held in high esteem, feared as much for their fighting prowess as for their writ of holy law. In 1377, Bishop Reede of Chichester built the great curtain wall and massive gatehouse that dominate the landscape today, and over the next few centuries, his successors altered and expanded it.

With the departure of the Bishops of Chichester the castle passed to the Crown. It was later caught up in the drama of the Civil War, when, following his defeat at the Battle of Worcester in 1651, Charles II took shelter there prior to heading for Shoreham and exile.

Purchased in 1893 by the then Duke of Norfolk, the castle remained in private hands and hidden from public view, until 1989, when it became a luxurious country hotel. Obviously a building of such glorious antiquity has had ample opportunity to acquire a resident ghost. Amberley's most famous harks back to those distant times when bishops

ABOVE: Wander among the stairways and passages of Farnham Castle at your peril, for many visitors have been terrified by a stern-faced spectre.

PREVIOUS PAGES: On a night like this, beneath the Roman walls of Pevensey Castle, William the Conqueror's army camped on their first night in England in 1066.

could plunder and pillage with impunity. In the castle kitchen in the 1300s, there, worked a serving wench, who is remembered simply as Emily. This poor girl was powerless to reject the lustful attentions of the then bishop, and as a result found herself with child. The holy hypocrite deserted her and left her to die in excruciating pain during childbirth.

Ever since, her ghost has returned to the castle, a sad, despondent shade, content to keep a mournful eye on the comings and goings below from the lofty heights of the castle walls.

PEVENSEY CASTLE
Pevensey, East Sussex Ⓐ Ⓔ
THE FEARLESS LADY PELHAM

Bracing its solid bulk against the ceaseless onslaught of the elements, its looming towers rising against the scudding clouds, Pevensey Castle is nothing less than a ruined testimony to bygone power. Constant threat of invasion from both land and sea caused successive owners to build for strength rather than for any other consideration. The castle has been besieged four times in its chequered past, without its enemies once managing to breach the defences. This speaks volumes about the sheer might of the battle-scarred walls that are blazoned with 17 centuries of history.

The sprawling and impressive outer walls are all that remain of the Roman fort of Anderida, which was built between AD280 and 340 to protect southern Britain against raids by Saxon pirates. When the Romans left, it seems that a community chose to reside here, for the *Anglo-Saxon Chronicle* records how, in AD491, a Saxon raiding party besieged the settlement and slaughtered every man, woman and child. Thereafter, the fort disappears from historical records for almost six centuries until, on 28th September 1066, William, Duke of Normandy arrived in Pevensey Bay to lay claim to the throne of England. Legend states that as the Duke leapt ashore he stumbled and fell.

Realizing that his army might interpret this as a bad omen, William quickly sprang to his feet and, waving aloft fistfuls of earth, cried to his men, 'I have seized this land in both hands and I will never let it go'.

That night, the Normans camped within the walls of the old Roman fort, and next morning, set out across the marshes to begin their invasion. On 14th October 1066, William defeated the English King Harold at the Battle of Hastings, and granted Pevensey to his half-brother, Robert of Mortain.

The castle that Robert built within the old Roman walls became one of the most important in southern England, and was never once stormed. The most famous of its sieges occurred in 1399, and may well have been responsible for the pale lady that is known to haunt Pevensey. In 1394, John of Gaunt, the 2nd Duke of Lancaster (1340–99) appointed Sir John Pelham as Constable of Pevensey Castle. Following John of Gaunt's death in 1399, Richard II seized the Duchy of Lancaster. This provoked the duke's exiled son, Henry Bolingbroke (1366–1413), to head for England to win back his inheritance and topple Richard from the throne. Sir John Pelham threw his support behind Henry and set off to fight alongside him. During his absence, a Yorkist army besieged the castle, and its defence fell to the constable's wife, Joan. At the height of the siege she managed to smuggle a letter to her husband informing him of her plight. 'My dear Lord,' she wrote, 'I am here laid in manner of a siege... Wherefore my dear may it please you, by the advice of your wise council, to give remedy to the salvation of your castle.' She held the enemy at bay until receipt of her letter brought John Pelham galloping to the relief of the garrison. On 29th September 1399, Richard II was persuaded to abdicate, and Bolingbroke was declared King Henry IV.

The anguish of the siege lingers at Pevensey Castle still and many people have seen the misty form of a pale lady gazing anxiously from the upper walls. It is believed, though not proven, that the forlorn phantom is that of Lady Joan Pelham whose spirit has been trapped by the trauma of those angst-filled

WINDSOR CASTLE
Windsor, Berkshire Ⓐ
GHOSTLY QUEENS, TRAGIC KINGS AND FLEETING SHADOWS

Windsor Castle was originally one of the chain of castles flung up by William the Conqueror as he attempted to subjugate the vanquished Anglo-Saxons. Over the ensuing centuries, it was continually added to, and now has the distinction of being both the oldest and largest inhabited castle in Europe.

As you approach the castle you are greeted by an elegant statue of Queen Victoria, placed here in 1887 to commemorate her Golden Jubilee. It has long been rumoured that Victoria held several séances at the castle in an attempt to contact the spirit of her consort, Prince Albert, whose death in 1861 had left her bereft. It is also claimed that she used her faithful retainer, John Brown, as her medium and that she kept copious notes of these endeavours. These records were reputedly discovered after her death by the Dean of Windsor, who burnt them for fear that they might cause a royal scandal should their contents ever be made public.

In February 1897, Lieutenant Carr Glyn of the Grenadier Guards was sitting reading in the outer room of the queen's library, when a lady dressed in black walked past him, and turned a corner. Intrigued by the fact that she reminded him of the portraits he had seen of Elizabeth I, Glynn followed, but could find no trace of her. Furthermore, there was no doorway through which she could have left the library. He asked an attendant who the lady was, but was told that he was the only person who had entered the library that afternoon. The attendant then raised the possibility that the lieutenant had been honoured with a spectral sighting of Queen Elizabeth I.

Elizabeth I is not the only royal to undertake ghostly perambulations around the corridors and grounds of Windsor Castle, for apparitions of both Henry VIII and Charles I have also been seen here. It was just before Christmas 1648 that Charles Stuart was taken as a prisoner to Windsor Castle following the decision that he should be 'prosecuted for his life as a criminal person'. Following his trial and beheading in

ABOVE: Where the Elizabethan manor house known as Bruce Castle stands today may once have been the site of a castle built by the father of Scotland's Robert the Bruce.

London on 30th January 1649, his body was returned to Windsor to be buried in the same vault as Henry VIII and Jane Seymour. As the black-draped coffin was being carried towards

St George's Chapel, the sky, which until then had been 'serene and clear', clouded over and a sudden blizzard swept across the grounds. The black pall over the coffin was 'all white' by the time they reached the end of the chapel, and many took this as a divine sign proclaiming the king's innocence.

As a sick old man, George III spent much of his time at Windsor, and each day would take and return the afternoon salute of his guards. Following his death, while his body still lay in state, the guards were passing the king's window when the commanding officer saw the unmistakable figure of the king standing in his customary place. Instinctively he gave the order 'Eyes right', and as they swung round each soldier saw the figure and watched as he returned their salute.

In April 1906, a sentry was on duty one night at the top of the pathway beyond the main entrance to the castle when a group of men appeared from nowhere, and began walking towards him. Thinking they were intruders the sentry challenged them, but they continued to advance. When they ignored his third challenge, he cocked his rifle and fired at the leading figure, which paused momentarily but then continued forward. Raising his bayonet, the soldier charged at the group,

ABOVE: Windsor Castle started life as one of a chain of defences built by William the Conqueror, and became Europe's oldest, largest and most haunted inhabited castle.

whereupon they promptly vanished into thin air. He reported the experience to his commanding officer and a full-scale search of the castle and grounds was undertaken, but no intruders were found and the sentry was confined to barracks for three days as punishment.

The view of the castle's south façade from the Long Walk in Windsor Great Park is stunning, although at night it can be sinister. It was here in 1927 that an 18-year-old guardsman, patrolling this area at night, was overcome with melancholy and shot himself. Some weeks later a colleague of his, Sergeant Leake, was given the same night duty. At the end of his shift, he was pleased to hear the footsteps of what he presumed to be his relief. Instead, he found himself gazing at the face of the young suicide. As he stood staring in astonishment, the genuine relief marched into view and the apparition vanished. Back at barracks, he reported his experience to several other sentries who all claimed to have witnessed manifestations of their dead associate.

DONNINGTON CASTLE
Nr Newbury, Berkshire ® Ⓔ
THE CASTLE THAT WOULDN'T SURRENDER

Donnington Castle's towering gatehouse, standing on a high spur and overlooking the old London-to-Bath road, is an awesome edifice that commands attention much as it has done since its construction in 1386. Built by Richard de Abberbury, chamberlain to Richard II's queen, Anne of Bohemia, its most eventful period was during the Civil War when Charles I seized it from its owner, John Packer, and appointed John Boys commander of the garrison.

In July 1644, the Parliamentarian General Middleton arrived with 3,000 men and demanded that the garrison surrender. When Boys refused, Middleton launched an ill-conceived siege that not only failed to break through the castle's defences but also cost him a tenth of his force. In September, a new force under a new commander loosed a 12-day volley of cannon fire at the walls. Three of the castle's flanking towers were blown to smithereens and the curtain wall was breeched, but still the valiant Boys refused to surrender. A month later, the Parliamentarians tried again and bombarded the castle with more than 1,000 shots. When they sent word demanding that Boys submit, they received short shrift. Then word arrived that Charles I was on his way to relieve the defenders and the attackers retreated. The exhausted garrison was reprovisioned and was able to enjoy a brief respite from hostilities.

When the second Battle of Newbury ended in stalemate on 28th October 1644, another assault on the castle led by Sir William Waller ensued. Once more, the demands for surrender were met with an emphatic 'no' from the gallant Boys, and a week later, a Royalist force commanded by Prince Rupert managed to relieve the garrison.

Colonel Boys used the respite afforded by the winter months to strengthen his defences and was once more prepared to continue his valiant stand. But the Civil War was drawing to a close. In March 1646, the Parliamentarians again demanded his surrender, so Boys sought the king's instructions and was told to get the best terms he could. On the 1st April 1646, having withstood almost 20 months of constant siege, John Boys surrendered to his adversaries. Parliament then voted for the demolition of the castle as it had become a symbol of valiant resistance. Today, all that remains are the twin towers of the mighty gatehouse, rising from the grassy hillside to a commanding 20 metres (65 feet).

Needless to say, such a turbulent history has resulted in several ghosts. There are persistent reports of a spectral white dog that comes bounding down the hill from the castle towards the woods below. The creature makes no sound, and the first intimation that he is anything other than living flesh and blood is when he suddenly vanishes into thin air. A ghostly guard has also been seen around the gatehouse. Whether he is the shade of one of the castle's Civil War defenders is unknown, since he never stays around long enough for witnesses to ask him! One minute he'll be standing by the gatehouse, a solid and apparently human figure, the next he will suddenly disappear, as one witness put it, 'like a bubble bursting'.

BELOW: The soaring bulk of Donnington Castle's gatehouse looms over its surroundings, while the thick walls crackle with the memories of past deeds.

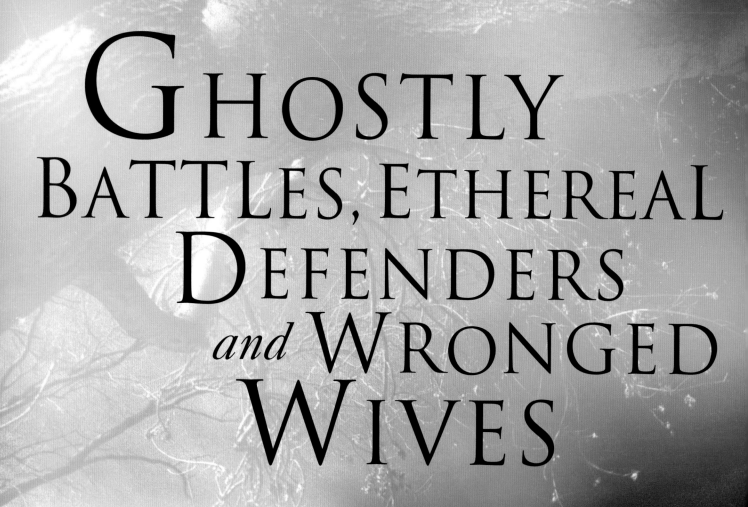

GHOSTLY BATTLES, ETHEREAL DEFENDERS and WRONGED WIVES

Soldier, rest! thy warfare o'er,
Sleep the sleep that knows not breaking;
Dream of battled fields no more,
Days of danger, nights of waking.
In our isle's enchanted hall,
Hands unseen thy couch are strewing,
Fairy strains of music fall,
Every sense in slumber dewing.

FROM *THE LADY OF THE LAKE*
BY SIR WALTER SCOTT (1771-1832)

SURREY, WEST SUSSEX, EAST SUSSEX & KENT

For centuries, the south-east corner of England was the gateway through which passed successive waves of invaders. Celts, Romans, Saxons, Angles, Jutes, Vikings and Normans all came this way. Moving inland, they built fortresses to protect themselves against the next possible invaders, and remnants of their defences still lie scattered across the landscape. Dover Castle's towering walls have commanded the road to London since the days of the Normans, while Scotney, Leeds, Hever and Bodiam are as romantic and tranquil castles as you could ever wish to find. By contrast, the soaring ramparts of Rochester Castle and the sprawling walls of Pevensey were built for defence rather than for prestige, and are still as awe-inspiring today as ever they were in their stormy past. The ghosts that haunt these places include Anne Boleyn, a spectral dog, ghostly Roman soldiers and that staple of the spectral landscape, the 'White Lady'.

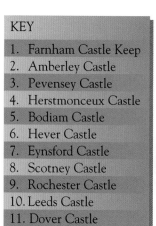

KEY

1. Farnham Castle Keep
2. Amberley Castle
3. Pevensey Castle
4. Herstmonceux Castle
5. Bodiam Castle
6. Hever Castle
7. Eynsford Castle
8. Scotney Castle
9. Rochester Castle
10. Leeds Castle
11. Dover Castle

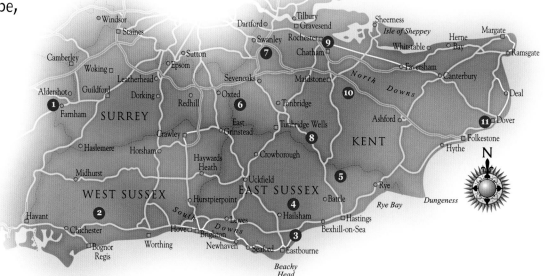

FARNHAM CASTLE KEEP
Farnham, Surrey Ⓐ Ⓔ
SPECTRAL REBUKE OF THE STERN-FACED LADY

A mysterious element emanates from the sombre ruin of Farnham Castle keep, which, from its imposing hilltop location casts mysterious shadows across the town of Farnham below. Originally built around 1138 by Henry de Blois,

Bishop of Winchester and brother of King Stephen, it was pulled down in 1154, when Stephen's successor, Henry II, set about righting the devastation wrought by the weak reign of his predecessor – 'a time when Christ and his saints slept' according to one chronicler.

Rebuilt, possibly by Henry de Blois himself, it remained a residential palace of the Bishops of Winchester until the early 20th century. Many visitors have reported sighting an indistinct and hazy form drifting about the ruins of the keep, to the terror of some of them. But only occasionally

OPPOSITE TOP: A luxury hotel now occupies Amberley Castle where a lustful bishop once held court.

OPPOSITE BOTTOM: King Charles II of England, who set out from Amberley Castle for France and exile.

ABOVE: The anguish of the victims of a siege at Pevensey Castle in the 14th century lingers still in the form of a pale lady who gazes out from the upper walls.

days, when she would scan the horizon seeking a distant speck that might signal her husband's approach and the end of her ordeal.

HERTSMONCEUX CASTLE

Hertsmonceux, East Sussex Ⓐ Ⓣ

THE PHANTOM DRUMMER

Sir Roger de Fiennes built this imposing castle in 1441. Today it is owned by the Queen's University of Kingston, Ontario, and its soaring red-brick walls, lofty turrets and deep moat - the result of a massive restoration in the early 20th century -

are every inch the haunted castle of tradition. There is a tale that one of Sir Roger's sons attempted to force himself upon one of the girls from the village, but met with valiant resistance. She escaped his clutches by leaping into the moat, but her attacker managed to catch hold of her and drag her back into the castle where he assaulted and then murdered her. This unfortunate girl is thought to be the spectral White Lady, whose noiseless wraith has been seen swimming desperately across the moat at night, or standing nearby, wringing her shrivelled hands in sorrowful torment.

The most famous shade to stir within the ancient walls is the Phantom Drummer, who has been seen striding along the ramparts at night. Some say that he lived in the 15th century and that he was killed at the Battle of Agincourt. Ever since he has beaten his own death tattoo, with showers of blue sparks cascading from his glowing drum sticks. Other accounts name him as Lord Dacre who, for some reason, pretended to have died but lived secretly in the castle with his beautiful young wife. To deter the attentions of the numerous suitors who came to woo his supposed widow, he donned a drummer's uniform, applied a liberal coating of phosphorous to his face, clothes and drum, and appeared as a fiendish phantom around the castle. His wife is said to have eventually grown so tired of his deceit that she locked him in his room, and starved him to death. Angered at the indignity of his ignominious demise, his ghost has patrolled the castle and grounds ever since.

BODIAM CASTLE
Bodiam, East Sussex Ⓐ 🌰
THE PHANTOM PARTY THAT NEVER ENDS

Bodiam, the quintessential medieval castle, nestles peacefully amid grassy fields, its ghostly image rippling in the silent waters of its lily-starred moat. Built by Sir Edward Dalyngrigge in 1385, the castle was intended both as a defence against a possible French invasion and, perhaps more importantly, an opulent testimony to the wealth and power of its owner. In the centuries that followed, the castle enjoyed a tranquil and relatively uneventful existence until, during the Civil War, its bridge and interior were dismantled and its barbican partly demolished to render it untenable. Thereafter, the ivy-clad ruins became a magnet to those who viewed it as a picturesque reminder of England's medieval glories. It was acquired in 1916 by Lord Curzon who, determined that 'so rare a treasure should neither be lost to our country nor desecrated by irreverent hands', bequeathed it to the National Trust. Today, it is a secret and romantic place whose ancient walls, weathered by a rustic hue, exude an atmosphere of such charm and tranquillity that several past residents seem loath to depart, and choose to linger here as spirits.

Some people passing the ruins at dead of night have reported the distinctive sound of spectral revels emanating from the hollow shell. Others have told of hearing 'strange oaths' and 'foreign-sounding songs'. Finally, there is the mysterious shade of a ghostly red lady, sometimes seen gazing from one of the towers, her eyes fixed upon some distant object, although what it is, and who she was, nobody knows.

HEVER CASTLE
Hever, Kent Ⓐ
THE GHOSTLY WALK OF ANNE BOLEYN

Hever is a castle in miniature. It possesses a grand dining hall that is a mere 12 metres (40 feet) long; a diminutive maze and exquisite Italian garden. The courtyard is more befitting that of an English country inn and the interior is one that any stately home would be proud of, resplendent with period furnishings, works of art and historic treasures. If none of these are reason enough to visit, there is the possibility of a chance encounter with the ghost of Anne Boleyn.

In 1460, Hever Castle came into the possession of wealthy London merchant Henry Bullen. It was his son, Thomas, who in

OPPOSITE: The moated Hertsmonceux Castle underwent massive restoration in the 20th century, but it is still haunted by a phantom drummer.

BELOW: An old engraving captures the spooky atmosphere of the 14th-century Bodiam Castle.

a concerted attempt at family aggrandizement, changed his surname to the more courtly 'Boleyn'. His daughter Anne returned to Hever from France in 1521 and first met Henry VIII in the castle garden a year later.

In 1525, Henry began an affair with Anne's sister, Mary. When Mary and her husband, William Carey, had a son the following year, whom they named Henry, court gossip was rife concerning the boy's paternity. Thus, when Henry's lusting eye focused on Mary's younger sister, the king expected little more than a token resistance. The strong-willed Anne, however, had other ideas. If Henry wanted her, he would have to marry her, and thus began a game of chase in which the king, for once, was forced to fight for his quarry. Henry wrote 17 letters to Anne, pledging himself, 'in heart body and will' her 'loyal and most ensured servant'. Consumed with passion he wrote how he wished himself 'in my

> 'SO RARE A TREASURE SHOULD NEITHER BE LOST TO OUR COUNTRY NOR DESECRATED BY IRREVERENT HANDS.'
>
> LORD CURZON ON BEQUEATHING BODIAM CASTLE TO THE NATIONAL TRUST

sweetheart's arms, whose pretty dukkys I facest shortly to kiss'.

Henry began his attempts to divorce Catherine of Aragon, and created Anne Marchioness of Pembroke. She travelled with the royal retinue and was given her own apartments. Finally, secure in the knowledge that the king was hers, she surrendered to his advances, and by the time she and Henry were secretly married in January 1533, Anne was pregnant. In the June of that year, her ambitions were realized when Archbishop Cranmer placed the crown on her head and declared her Henry's queen. It was a universally unpopular coronation. As far as most people were concerned Anne was a witch who had seduced the king, and whose unforgivable actions had resulted in a dreadful rift between Church and State. In September Anne gave birth to a daughter. Henry, who had long hoped for a son and heir, was

disappointed yet not despairing, and the girl was christened Elizabeth. When each of Anne's next pregnancies ended in miscarriage, the king's ardour began to cool and he found solace in the arms, and bed, of one of her maids of honour, Jane Seymour. He began paying attention to the gossip spread by Anne's

ABOVE: Every Christmas Eve, the beautiful grounds of Hever Castle are visited by Anne Boleyn, the once-loved and thereafter rejected wife of King Henry VIII.

BELOW: King Henry VIII of England, whose despotic actions helped swell the country's ghostly populace.

detractors, and on 2nd May 1536 she was arrested and charged with treasonous adultery and incest with her own brother. Anne was sent to the Tower of London, declared guilty and sentenced to death. On 19th May 1536, she was beheaded at the Tower of London.

Anne's father, Thomas Boleyn retired to Hever Castle in disgrace. Following his death in 1538, Henry commandeered the property and later gave it to Anne of Cleves, whom he had just divorced. Thereafter, Hever fell into disrepair, even being used as a farmhouse at one stage. It was bought in 1903 by the American multi-millionaire William Waldorf Astor, who set about a restoration project that saw 2,000 workmen labour continuously for four years to create the jewel that greets visitors today.

Inevitably, Anne Boleyn haunts Hever Castle, Christmas Eve being her chosen day. Her sombre spectre is seen drifting silently over the picturesque bridge that spans the river Eden, in the grounds of the home where she knew much happiness, and from which she embarked upon a journey that would change the course of English history.

EYNSFORD CASTLE
Eynsford, Kent Ⓔ
THE HAUNTED RUBBLE

There is a theory that buildings can somehow record the events that have happened within them, and that walls can become charged with the energy, personalities and emotions of those who have lived there. Being one of the earliest examples of a stone enclosure castle in England, the coarse flint rubble of Eynsford Castle, built by William de Eynsford in 1088, has had almost 1,000 years in which to accumulate a veritable library of sensations.

Many people who visit the ruins have commented on a certain 'cold spot' at a particular place in the moat, which now stands empty. It may be a warm summer's day and the rest of the castle might bask in brilliant sunshine, but at this location the air is always icy cold.

Over the years, parts of the castle have been incorporated into other buildings in the village, one of which is now the studio of this book's photographer, John Mason. Several times, some mischievous sprite has rearranged the furniture and equipment there. John has returned from overseas shoots to be told by neighbours that the heavy main door (the only set of keys to which he had with him) was heard slamming repeatedly, although when investigated they found it to be firmly locked. Friends staying overnight at the studio have

ABOVE: The plain, early stone enclosure design of Eynsford Castle has been enlivened by some very disturbing noises and sensations.

woken the next morning to find their clothes hanging over the rafters. Two models who were having a heated argument during a shoot were astonished when a heavy box was flung across the room. Whether or not the ghostly goings-on are the result of some force or emotion transferred to the studio in the rubble of the castle is pure speculation. Interestingly, the activity always seems to occur in the vicinity of the only wall that is built from the remnants of Eynsford Castle.

SCOTNEY CASTLE
Nr Lamberhurst, Kent Ⓐ 🌰
A BEDRAGGLED SPECTRE COMES A-KNOCKING

Ensconced within a tall screen of leafy boughs, and shielded from prying eyes by a picturesque profusion of flora and fauna, the dreamy ruins of Scotney Castle blend harmoniously into their surroundings. No one who ventures here can deny that the whole foundation lies in a time warp.

Roger Ashburnham built Scotney Castle between 1378 and 1380, in response to the potential threat of a French invasion. Later it came into the possession of the staunchly Papist Darell

family, who allowed the Jesuit priest, Richard Blount, to use their home as a base and hiding place during the Catholic persecutions in the reign of Elizabeth I. At Christmas 1598, the authorities, having received a tip-off concerning his whereabouts, arrived to search the castle. As Father Blount hid within the priest's hole (which can still be seen inside the castle today), Mistress Darrell noticed that his belt was protruding from beneath the secret door. By way of a warning to the hidden cleric, she raised her voice slightly. The searching soldiers noticed this and, convinced that they were close to their quarry, began to batter down the outside wall, and would certainly have found him had not a thunderstorm halted their search. It was imperative that the priest should escape, and a cunning plan was duly hatched. As the soldiers (who had moved into the castle to facilitate a more thorough search) dined that night, a servant burst into the room and told them that someone was stealing their horses. When the troops rushed out, Richard Blount crept from his hiding place, swam across the moat and vanished into the night, never to be captured.

In the mid 17th century, William Darell demolished much of the old castle and used its stone to build the magnificent east range, the romantic ruin of which is one of the glories of the castle garden today. In 1720 Arthur Darell, then owner of the castle, died abroad, and his body was brought back for burial in nearby Lamberhurst Church. As the coffin was being lowered into the grave, those present noticed a stranger, swathed in a long black cloak, standing among them. As the service neared its conclusion, the mysterious figure turned to a fellow mourner and whispered: 'That is me they think they are burying!' Moments later he had disappeared and, despite a thorough search, no sign of him could be found. Did the ghost of Arthur Darell appear at his own funeral, or was there a more earthly explanation behind the bizarre incident? It has been suggested that Arthur may well have faked his own death to free himself from the baleful pursuit of his litigious sisters who resented the fact that he had inherited the family estate. With Arthur's death, the castle passed to a kinsman whom the sisters harried mercilessly in a series of frenzied and expensive lawsuits that all but bankrupted the estate. Arthur, meanwhile, used the cover of his supposed death to set himself up as a smuggler, living a secret existence in the grounds of Scotney. One day an excise officer almost caught him, but Arthur murdered the man and flung his body into the moat. Thereafter he fled the estate and vanished. Ever since there have been frequent reports of a bedraggled figure that staggers from the moat and moves slowly towards the old castle where, having knocked soundlessly upon the door, it melts away into thin air.

ROCHESTER CASTLE
Rochester, Kent Ⓐ Ⓔ
THE WHITE LADY'S LOFTY DOMAIN

The great keep of Rochester Castle, one of the largest such structures in England, is a forbidding fortress that still dominates the Medway, as it has done for almost a 1,000 years. Built by William de Corbeil, Archbishop of Canterbury in the early years of the 12th century, it remained under the authority of his successors until 1215, when King John laid siege to it for seven weeks. The King's forces battered the garrison into submission with a constant barrage of hefty rocks launched from five massive catapults, accompanied by an endless volley of crossbow bolts. The castle was again besieged in 1264, when Simon

'THAT IS ME THEY THINK THEY ARE BURYING!'

ARTHUR DARELL AT HIS OWN FUNERAL

de Montfort rebelled against Henry III.

In de Montfort's army was a knight named Gilbert de Clare. He was the rejected suitor of Lady Blanche de Warenne, who was now holed up inside the castle with her fiancé Sir Ralph de Capo. A week of battering by stone-throwing machines caused heavy damage to the castle. A mine tunnel was then begun which would have toppled the walls and brought about the castle's capture had not de Montford been forced to beat a hasty retreat when news was brought that the king was approaching with an army. Suddenly, the castle gates opened and Sir Ralph, emboldened by the proximity of the king's forces, led his fellow defenders in pursuit of the retreating rebels. Lady Blanche de Warenne watched the skirmish from the southern battlements of the castle and, no doubt, felt a twinge of relief when she saw her betrothed galloping back towards its gates. Unfortunately, it was in fact the dastardly Sir Gilbert de Clare who, having donned an identical surcoat to that worn by Sir Ralph, was able to ride unchallenged into the castle, and climb to the ramparts where he seized Lady Blanche. At that moment, Sir Ralph looked up from the

fighting and saw his lover struggling against a vicious assault. He seized an archer's bow, took aim, and fired an arrow high into the air. Tragically, it glanced off de Clare's armour and killed Blanche. That night her ghost was seen walking upon the battlements, the arrow still protruding from her. And she has walked her timeworn path ever since, a forlorn figure, whose dark hair, streaming in the breeze, provides a vivid contrast to the brilliant white of her dress.

LEEDS CASTLE
Leeds, Kent Ⓐ
THE BLACK DOG OF LEEDS

This fairytale stronghold is one of the most beautiful castles in England. It stands on two islands surrounded by a tranquil lake, and has seen much English history wash around its walls. The current castle was begun in the mid 13th century, but was handed over to Edward I in lieu of certain debts, by its then owner, William of Leybourne. Edward II besieged the castle in 1321, when Bartholomew of Badlesmere, holding it as a gift of the monarch, refused entry to Queen Isabella of France, wife of Edward II. Richard II was imprisoned at Leeds, and it has been home to so many royal wives that it is called the 'castle of the medieval Queens of England'.

Continuously added to by successive owners, a good proportion of what survives today was built as recently as 1822, by which time the old fortress had acquired the ghostly black dog, whose appearances often presaged bad luck, or even death for the occupants. Its origins are said to lie in the demonic dabbling of Henry VI's aunt, Eleanor of Gloucester, who in 1431 was found guilty of practising 'necromancy, witchcraft, heresy and treason' and was imprisoned at Leeds Castle for the rest of her life. Perhaps the hound results from some ancient spell cast by this formidable lady, and which has lingered around property ever since.

DOVER CASTLE
Dover, Kent Ⓐ Ⓔ
A SPECTRAL CORNUCOPIA AND A PLUMMETING PHANTOM

Few British fortresses can boast a pedigree as impressive as that of Dover Castle. It gazes seaward from a lofty vantage point, hurling its defiant challenge at all would-be invaders: 'Topple me if you can!'

Much of the structure that confronts today's visitor was built by order of Henry II (1133–89). One of the most stirring events in its history occurred in 1216, during the reign of Henry's universally despised son, King John (1167–1216). The Pope, having failed to subjugate John with spiritual threats, called on Louis of France to depose him. Louis arrived with a French army equipped with several engines of war and, having joined forces with the English barons, laid siege to Dover Castle. Its walls held for 15 weeks, before the death of John intervened to change English attitudes and turn opinion against the Frenchman, forcing him to return home.

Centuries later, when Dover became an important defence against another possible French invasion during the Napoleonic Wars, a young drummer boy was reputedly murdered in the labyrinth of subterranean passages which are beneath the castle. Presumably his assailants decapitated their victim, for the phantom strolls along the battlements without

its head. Within the solid walls of the old keep, a woman in a flowing red dress shares her ethereal domain with a male spectre in the garb of a cavalier. The underground tunnels, formerly known as Hellfire Corner, are where witnesses have reported seeing the shades of several World War II personnel. They are also where an American couple heard screams and cries, which they considered to be impressively realistic sound effects, until told by staff that there were no such re-creations at the castle.

Invisible whispering voices, heard in the dead of night, doors opening and closing of their own volition, and sudden drops in temperature for no earthly reason, are just some of the other phenomena experienced at the castle. If none of this is sufficient to elicit cold shivers, then heed the experience of two television researchers who, while walking past the keep, heard a scream from above, as though someone had just flung

themselves from the battlements. Convinced that a suicide was plummeting towards them, they leapt for cover and waited for the impact. Moments later, the screams ceased — but no body made contact with *terra firma*.

OPPOSITE BOTTOM: A black hound presaging death mars the exquisite beauty of Leeds Castle, set as it is, on two picturesque islands in a serene lake.

RIGHT: Dover Castle, a soaring symbol of medieval defiance at the south-eastern edge of England, is also the realm of many phantoms, including one of a cavalier.

Sea-sprayed Ramparts, Hellish Hounds and the Devil's Nimble Footwork

As I sat musing, 'twas a host in dank array,
With their horses and their cannon wheeling onward to the fray,
Moving like a shadow to the fate the brave must dree,
And behind me roared the drums, rang the trumpets of the sea.

FROM *THE SONG OF SOLDIERS*
BY WALTER DE LA MARE (1873–1956)

ESSEX, SUFFOLK NORFOLK & CAMBRIDGESHIRE

The eastern counties of England occupy the area that once formed the ancient Kingdom of East Anglia. Bound to the west by the swamps of the Fens, buffered to the east and north by the sea, and hemmed in at the south by the thick woodlands of Saxon Essex, it was for centuries an aloof and mysterious region, populated by a hard and resourceful but superstitious people. Successive waves of invaders did manage to breach the region's natural defences and Romans, Angles, Saxons, Vikings and Danes have all left their mark upon the landscape. The more peaceful incursions of Icelandic fishermen, Flemish weavers and Dutch drainage specialists have in turn left an imprint on the region's trades, skills and agriculture. The ghosts that wander around many of the ruined castles hereabouts reflect the changing demographics of the region. Their amazing stories reflect the beliefs and cultures that the successive waves of settlers brought with them and supplanted into their new habitats. Demon hounds, royal wraiths and nebulous nobles all inhabit a spectral domain in which myths and legends bond, and infamous acts are often re-enacted by phantom protagonists before astonished witnesses.

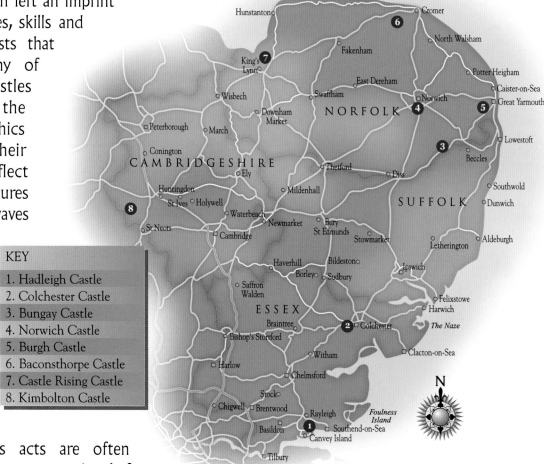

KEY

1. Hadleigh Castle
2. Colchester Castle
3. Bungay Castle
4. Norwich Castle
5. Burgh Castle
6. Baconsthorpe Castle
7. Castle Rising Castle
8. Kimbolton Castle

HADLEIGH CASTLE
Hadleigh, Essex Ⓡ Ⓔ
THE DEVIL'S JIG
AMONG THE RUINS

Little now remains of Hadleigh Castle save a handful of mouldering walls and a shattered round tower. Begun in 1230 by Hubert de Burgh, building work came to an abrupt halt when, following a violent quarrel, Henry III attempted to stab his former Regent in a fit of rage, and then confiscated his unfinished castle. Henry continued the construction, as did Edward III, who made considerable additions in the 14th century.

It became customary for Hadleigh Castle to be granted to a tenant for life, on the understanding it would revert to the Crown following the death of the occupier. Traditionally these residents were royal consorts, most notably three of Henry VIII's wives: Catherine of Aragon, Anne of Cleves and Catherine Parr. Following Henry's death, Edward VI sold the property on condition that it be demolished and the stone used for building work elsewhere.

In the 18th century, stories began circulating that ghosts had been seen flitting about the ragged vestiges at dead of night. It must be said that smugglers invented many of these tales as they went about their nefarious business, in order to keep the superstitious locals away. To this end ,they would also burn coloured lights to convince the nearby residents that evil spirits were at large on the windswept hilltop.

The smugglers have long since departed, but people continue to experience encounters with strange ethereal forms among the ruins. The most frequent is the White Lady, whom tradition has bestowed with a fearsome reputation. Should she discover you in her domain at night, she will compel you to dance. Round and round you will swirl, until you drop exhausted to the ground, whereupon the devil will appear, to claim your soul for eternity.

ABOVE: The overgrown fragments of Hadleigh Castle are haunted by a dancing phantom of evil intent.

PREVIOUS PAGES: Standing on the site of the Roman Temple of Claudius, and in medieval times, the focus of many a witch hunt, Colchester Castle's long and history has begotten many a spectre.

LEFT: Inside the walls of Colchester Castle a most shameful act of injustice took place when the gentle Quaker James Parnell was cruelly imprisoned – until death.

OPPOSITE: Earth, grass and crumbling stone soften the image of Bungay Castle, but the black hound of hell lurks there by night.

town, Parnell left home in search of spiritual enlightenment, and travelled among the numerous religious sects that met in secret to avoid persecution. In so doing he met with a group that 'waited together in silence to be instruments in the hand of the lord'. He had discovered the Quakers. Having heard that George Fox, their founder, was imprisoned at that time at Carlisle Castle, Parnell walked 240 kilometres (150 miles) to visit him. Although little is known of their meeting, Parnell came away fully committed to the Quaker cause.

Travelling the country, he became a talented and committed preacher whose challenge to the established Church brought him into direct conflict with the authorities. On 12th July 1655, he arrived in Coggeshall, Essex, where the vicar was preparing to offer a special prayer 'against the errors of the Quakers'. Despite his small stature Parnell had a commanding presence, and held his audience enraptured as he vociferously argued against the vicar's views. By the end of that day he had been arrested and was imprisoned in Colchester Castle. At his subsequent trial, the jury would only convict him of 'writing a pamphlet', an 'offence' he freely admitted, and he was fined the hefty sum of £40. He refused to pay and was sent back to Colchester Castle.

The gaoler at the castle was a certain Nicholas Roberts, who was renowned for his cruel, corrupt and vindictive ways, and made strenuous efforts to break Parnell's spirit. He kept him in cramped, filthy conditions in a deep hole in the castle wall. To obtain the paltry rations of food afforded him Parnell had first to climb a rope suspended from the 3.5-metre (12-foot) high ceiling. Gradually his health broke down, his decline exacerbated by injuries sustained when he fell from the top of the rope. He was refused medical attention, and by April 1656 his appetite for both food and life was failing. On the night of 4th May 1656, James Parnell died, and his body was buried in an unmarked grave in the castle grounds.

There are reports of a small, thin, ghostly man who walks through a wall in one of the castle's lower dungeons. Some witnesses describe the figure as having a pronounced limp; others say that he just glides silently along the narrow

COLCHESTER CASTLE
Colchester, Essex Ⓐ
THE QUIVERING QUAKER

Colchester Castle has a history that is both fascinating and moving. There must be many a soul who, having had associations with the site, has ample cause to linger around it long after death. But it is the 17th-century Quaker James Parnell whose sufferings have, apparently, left their indelible mark upon the old and sturdy walls of this imposing fortress.

Parnell hailed from East Retford, Nottinghamshire, and grew up during the years that saw England racked by Civil War. It was a time when the country was in a state of religious turmoil, and thousands of pamphlets promoting a plethora of religious doctrines were in circulation. Dissatisfied with the priests of his corridors. Whichever, the sombre spirit at Colchester must be one of the most poignant, yet inspiring, of all England's castle ghosts. For James Parnell's courage in sacrificing everything for what he truly believed in remains a shining example to us all.

BUNGAY CASTLE
Bungay, Suffolk ®
THE HAUNT OF THE HOUND OF HELL

The combined effects of weather and time have left Bungay Castle tottering and in ruins. Green shoots sprout from the crumbling walls. Ivy clings fitfully to the once mighty towers, while carpets of grass and nettle cover the scant remnants of the upper floors. It is a solitary and secret place, capable of evoking shudders of inexplicable horror when the moon's dull glow starts weird shapes moving about the darker recesses. Then the ghost of one of its most feared former residents, Hugh Bigod, comes bounding from its past in the guise of one the most terrifying creatures ever to set foot on the Suffolk byways: Black Shuk, the demon hound.

Known as 'Bigod the Bold' and 'Bigod the Restless', Hugh Bigod was a warring though charismatic baron, who hailed from an illustrious Norman family. Having raised an army against King Stephen in 1136, he was besieged at Bungay by the Royalist forces. In the subsequent negotiations, Stephen awarded him the title of Earl of Suffolk, for no other reason than to win his future loyalty. Bigod showed his gratitude by raising another army. The next king, Henry II, confiscated the property but gave it back in 1163 when Bigod was no longer considered a threat. Thereafter this rebellious and quarrelsome baron spent ten years building the virtually impregnable stone keep of Bungay Castle. Emboldened by his new stronghold, he joined forces with the Earl of Leicester, and helped capture the royal castle at Haughley. However, when Henry II mustered a massive fighting force to meet the challenge, Hugh Bigod had little choice but to surrender. He was outlawed and forced to relinquish his properties to the Crown. Thereafter he departed for Syria where he died in 1178.

Such was his fearsome reputation that his spirit has long since been transmogrified into that hideous hound of hell, Black Shuk. Woe-betide anyone who, having been brave or foolish enough to venture here in the dead of night, chances upon this feared and fearsome beast. Luckily his victims are few and far between, for such is his reputation that even today people will not walk near the sombre ruins when darkness has fallen, and the wind laughs eerily from the crumbling crevices of the old castle.

Norwich Castle
Norwich, Norfolk Ⓐ
THE PHANTOM-SEEING FELONS

In 1087, William the Conqueror ordered one of his principle barons, William FitzOsberne, to build a castle at Norwich. A steep-sided artificial mound 12 metres (40 feet) high was dug, and a wooden fortress erected on top. Between 1120 and 1130, this was replaced by the impressive stone stronghold that dominates the city today. A hundred years later, the castle was designated as the Norfolk county gaol, in which capacity it continued for over 650 years until it was sold to the City of Norwich in 1887 and converted into a museum.

An incident in 1820 was apparently thought so extraordinary that it was considered worthy of mention in the gaol's journal. Three young men, who were awaiting transportation, were scared half out of their wits by a supernatural entity that appeared to them in the dead of night. Although being officially reported, this appears to have been a one-off haunting. Those who work at the newly refurbished museum today find the ghostly woman in the Victorian-style black dress who sometimes honours them with a visit anything but terrifying.

Burgh Castle
Nr Belton, Norfolk Ⓐ
THE FLYING CORPSE

Burgh Castle was actually the Roman fort of Gariannonum, built in the latter half of the 3rd century in response to the threat of attack by Saxon pirates. Its massive, flint-faced walls and toppled bastion are still truly awe-inspiring, and it is easy to see why people once believed that only giants could have

built such a place. When the Romans departed in the 5th century, Jutes, Danes and Norsemen arrived and began to settle in the area. Finally, a large band of Saxons found their way into the region and began migrating towards the area now known as Reedham. Their leader, Siberg, sent scouts ahead. They returned with the disturbing news that a ruthless and tyrannical Danish warlord, Gonard, occupied Gariannonum. Despite his peaceful intentions, Siberg knew that war with the Danes was inevitable. He despatched a messenger to his half-brother, Cerdag, whose tribe had already settled to the north of the Humber, asking that he come to his aid.

No sooner had the messenger left than Gonard sent an envoy inviting Siberg and his men to a meeting. Siberg, however, insisted on going alone, but before he left he told his people that if he had not returned within three days they must come to his rescue. So saying, he made his way to Gonard's fortress. The Dane instantly had Siberg clapped in irons and flung into a rat-infested dungeon, deep within the fort's foundations.

Four days later, Siberg's army arrived to free their leader. But the fortress's huge walls proved impregnable, and the assault both exhausted and demoralized them. Then, suddenly, two different gates opened, and the Danes attacked the Saxon rear and flank, inflicting a vicious rout. Surveying the corpse-littered battlefield, Gonard ordered his men to erect sharpened wooden posts all around the fortress. By dawn the next day, 4,000 dead and dying Saxons had been impaled on these stakes as a warning to anyone else who might consider challenging the Dane. A few days later Gonard was seated on

ABOVE: William the Conqueror, whose invasion of England sparked a boom in castle building that lasted for nearly 500 years.

LEFT: A white draped corpse plummets from the massive walls of Burgh Castle every year on 3rd July.

OPPOSITE: Time stands still among the secluded ruins of Baconsthorpe Castle in Norfolk.

the highest wall of his fortress, relishing the gruesome vista that surrounded him, when a strange vision appeared in the sky above. Two angels — one white, the other black — began doing battle. Back and forth they flew, each endeavouring to destroy the other. Finally the white angel clasped the black one by the throat, and the two plummeted earthwards, melting away as they fell. Troubled by this apparition, Gonard sent for Siberg, hoping that he might explain its meaning. Setting his long handled battleaxe before him, Gonard told Siberg what he had seen. At first Siberg said nothing; then a faint smile quivered upon his emaciated face and, raising a trembling finger, he pointed to the horizon. Turning to look, Gonard's jaw dropped at the sight of a vast army of Saxons moving towards him. 'That is the host of Cerdag, my kinsman,' sneered Siberg, 'and he has come to avenge the massacre of my people.' Then, before Gonard had chance to react, Siberg leapt forward, seized the battleaxe, and sunk it deep into the Dane's skull. His screams went unheeded as the Danish soldiers rushed to defend the fortress.

When his men had completely surrounded the fort, Cerdag sent a messenger, holding a white flag of truce, to demand that the garrison surrender. The defenders' contemptuous reply was to hurl the emissary's dead body from one of the parapets, the ensign tied around his neck in a strangle-knot. Cerdag gave the signal and his men raced forward and stormed the fortress, killing every one of Gonard's men. It was with grim satisfaction that Cerdag climbed to the highest wall to savour his victory. No sooner had he done so than he heard a deep sigh from behind a parapet wall. Stepping over the corpses to

investigate, he discovered his mortally wounded kinsman, Siberg. There was nothing he could do except hold him in his arms and comfort him until his laboured breathing ceased.

Thus is the legend of Burgh Castle, and so it is that on 3rd July each year, the corpse of the messenger, the white flag tied tightly round his neck, comes hurtling from the castle precincts and, having hit the ground with a sickening thud, vanishes into thin air.

BACONSTHORPE CASTLE
Baconsthorpe, Norfolk ®
THE CONTENTED SENTRY AND A PHANTOM 'PLOP'

There are castles that possess an almost dream-like quality, where time almost stops in its tracks. Such a place is Baconsthorpe Castle, built in the 15th century by Sir John Heydon. He was a self-seeking lawyer who made his fortune through mastering the dangerous art of switching his allegiance between the rival factions in the Wars of the Roses (1455–85). Over the next few centuries, the castle's fortunes rose and fell. After the Civil War, much of the castle was demolished, leaving behind the romantic ruin that nestles in peaceful seclusion, and which is reached via the tranquil back lanes of rural Norfolk. It has a sturdy, three-storeyed gatehouse, flanking towers along its walls, and is surrounded in part by a lake and in part by a moat. There has long been a legend that an underground passage runs under the moat

CASTLE RISING CASTLE

Castle Rising, Norfolk

Ⓐ Ⓔ

THE SHE-WOLF'S SPECTRAL DEMENTIA

Defensively situated atop its prodigious man-made earthworks of massive ramparts and deep ditches, Castle Rising Castle boasts an impressive pedigree that stretches back to 1140. Then it was that the magnificent Norman keep was built by William Albini to celebrate his marriage to the widow of Henry I. Over the next 400 years, it evolved into a magnificent residence. Following the execution of its owner, the Duke of Norfolk in 1572, the castle was abandoned. It deteriorated rapidly, its walls made precarious by a proliferation of rabbits burrowing into the earthen banks.

Today, the castle ruin is as impressive as ever, and is one of the largest and most ornate in England. Ascending the great stone staircase and passing into the keep one is greeted by an enigmatic maze of corridors and passageways which lead to a fascinating sequence of rooms, galleries and tiny staircases, where the upper rooms are said to be haunted by the ghost of one of the castle's most notorious former residents, Isabella, the 'she-wolf of France'.

As the former mistress of the power-hungry Roger Mortimer, she had been instrumental in the horrific murder (see page 81) of her husband Edward II in 1327. It is a widely held misconception that her son Edward III, following the execution of Mortimer, imprisoned her at the castle in 1331. Nothing could be further from the truth. Not only did Isabella live in regal splendour here, but she was also free to move with her retinue between her various residences as befitted a lady of her social standing. Legend, however, states that this formidable woman sank into an old age that was racked by violent dementia, her last troubled years being spent in the whitewashed rooms of the upper storeys. She died at her castle in Hertford on 23rd August 1358, and was buried in the monastery of the Greyfriars by Newgate in London.

The echoes of her last troubled years are still said to

from a turret in the castle. Sadly, recent excavations uncovered this subterranean tunnel and it transpired that it was a sewer that ended in the moat!

However, the sleepy ambience of the castle seems to have made it difficult for at least one former resident to leave. Many visitors have heard the sound of plopping, and on turning have discovered ripples radiating outwards across the glassy surface of the moat. Looking up, they see a ghostly sentry standing on the walls, lobbing 'plum stones' into the otherwise peaceful water. Quite who he is, no one knows. And since his spectral activity is undisruptive, witnesses are content to leave him be to enjoy his harmless fun.

rebound through the corridors of the Castle. Several visitors have been shocked by the sound of hysterical cackling around the top floor of the building. Residents in the nearby village have occasionally been disturbed by ghostly screams and maniacal laughter coming from the castle in the early hours of the morning.

KIMBOLTON CASTLE
Kimbolton, Cambridgeshire Ⓐ Ⓣ
RETURN OF THE QUEEN

Looking more like a stately home than a medieval stronghold, Kimbolton Castle is now a school, which occasionally opens its doors to allow visitors to view the impressive range of state rooms. The castle's most famous resident was Catherine of Aragon, the estranged wife of King Henry VIII, who arrived there in May 1534. She had been there for three weeks when Henry sent the Bishop of Durham to demand that she swear the oath acknowledging Henry as head of the Church in England and accept Anne Boleyn as queen. 'Hold thy peace, bishop!' she cried. 'These are the wiles of the devil! I am queen and queen I will die! By right, the king can have no other wife. Let this be your answer.'

When the bishop warned Catherine that her obstinacy might lead her to the scaffold she replied, 'And who will be the hangman? If you have permission to execute this penalty on me, I am ready. I ask only that I be allowed to die in sight of the people.' The bishop backed down and turned his attention to her household who surprised him by gladly swearing the oath in their native Spanish tongue, just as their mistress had instructed them: 'El Rey se ha heco cabeza de la Inglesia,' they intoned. The Bishop, not realizing that, instead of acknowledging the King as head of the Church, the servants had stated that he had made himself its head, departed satisfied.

However, many of Catherine's loyal supporters were convinced that the king wished her dead, and it was feared that she would be poisoned. She spent almost two years at Kimbolton Castle, her health declining with each passing day. On 1st December 1535, she fell seriously ill. Although she recovered, and was able to celebrate her 50th birthday, she suffered a relapse on 26th December, and by early January it was clear that she was dying. Too weak to write, she dictated a final letter to the king. Addressing him as 'My lord and dear husband' she wrote that 'The hour of my death draweth fast on' before beseeching him to 'Safeguard your soul, which you ought to prefer before any consideration of the world or flesh'. Finally, she traced a signature that symbolized all she had fought for: 'Catherine the Queen'. Early on the afternoon of 7th January 1536, Catherine of Aragon died. That evening, the castle's chandler carried out an autopsy and discovered that her heart 'had a black growth, all hideous to behold... and... when cut open the heart was black inside'. Modern medical opinion holds the view that Catherine died of a malignant heart tumour. But contemporary belief was convinced that Anne Boleyn had poisoned her. Even Henry VIII had his suspicions.

'Now I am indeed a queen,' observed a delighted Anne on receiving the news of Catherine's death. Henry's reaction was one of joyful relief, and on 9th January, he and Anne dressed in bright yellow silk and presided over a magnificent court ball to celebrate the fact that Catherine's death had liberated England from the threat of war with Spain. It was left then, to the people of England, to mourn her loss and remember her selflessness.

Catherine's ghost returns to the place where she spent her last austere and miserable years. A pale shade with a sad bearing, she drifts silently through what remains of the Tudor castle where her single-mindedness, personal courage and devotion to the husband who had so cruelly betrayed her still stand as a testimony to her sheer strength of character.

OPPOSITE: The demented spectre of Queen Isabella – 'The She-Wolf of France' – often terrifies visitors to Castle Rising Castle.

BELOW: Kimbolton Castle is now a school, but parts date from when Catherine of Aragon spent her final years there.

> ### 'I AM QUEEN AND QUEEN I WILL DIE!'
>
> CATHERINE OF ARAGON, REFUSING TO ACKNOWLEDGE HENRY VIII AS HEAD OF THE CHURCH

The END
of The Affair
and Wicked
Witches

SILENT is the house: all are laid asleep:
One alone looks out o'er the snow wreaths deep,
Watching every cloud, dreading every breeze
That whirls the wildering drift, and bends the groaning trees.

From The Visionary
by Emily Brontë (1818–48)

NORTHAMPTONSHIRE, LEICESTERSHIRE, NOTTINGHAMSHIRE & LINCOLNSHIRE

The counties that stretch inland from the Lincolnshire coast have, over the millennia, been home to sundry peoples, and are steeped in some of the best-known legends of English history. Celts, Romans and Vikings have all left their mark, both upon the varied landscape and the folk memory of the region, while numerous historical characters are associated with the area. On a forlorn mound in Northamptonshire, Scottish thistles still grow upon the site of Fotheringay Castle, where King Richard III was born, and where the execution of Mary, Queen of Scots, launched what is arguably Britain's most active revenant upon the spectral landscape. Leicestershire's Belvoir Castle was once the scene of a series of chilling events that tragically illustrate the prejudices and superstitions of the past, and Nottingham Castle is indelibly linked with the legend of Robin Hood. Elsewhere, the soaring redbrick tower of Tattershall Castle stands as proud testimony to political ambition, and Charles Dickens made his own unique contribution to our spectred isle when he saw the ghost of one of his own characters at Rockingham Castle.

KEY

1. Fotheringay Castle
2. Rockingham Castle
3. Belvoir Castle
4. Nottingham Castle
5. Lincoln Castle
6. Tattershall Castle

FOTHERINGAY CASTLE
Fotheringay, Northamptonshire Ⓢ
THE CURSE OF FOTHERINGAY AND QUEEN MARY'S TEARS

The heavy hand of disaster once fell with chilling regularity across the shoulders of those who had the misfortune to reside at the long-demolished Fotheringay Castle. Edward III (1312–77) rebuilt the Norman castle and granted it to his son Edward, Duke of York, who was subsequently killed at the Battle of Agincourt. It then came into the ownership of Richard Plantagenet, Earl of Cambridge, who was executed on 5th August 1415. The castle then passed to Richard, Duke of York, and it was here in 1452 that his wife Cicely gave birth to the future Richard III. For a time, the Duke appeared inured against the bad luck that had plagued previous owners. In 1454, he was even appointed Regent, ruling on behalf of Henry VI who had suffered a temporary bout of madness. On 31st

December 1460, the Duke of York was killed at the Battle of Wakefield along with his 18-year-old son, Edmund, Earl of Rutland. His elder son became King Richard III of England in 1483, but his reign was cut short when he was killed at the Battle of Bosworth in 1485.

Later, Henry VIII repaired the castle and awarded it to Catherine of Aragon as part of her dowry. It would have become her prison but she insisted she 'would not go unless bound with cart ropes and carried thither'. Instead, her last years were spent at Kimbolton Castle (see page 75). It was, however, both prison and place of execution for another tragic figure, Mary, Queen of Scots. Here she was tried for treason, and in the Great Hall on 8th February 1587, she was beheaded.

In the 17th century, Fotheringay Castle was demolished and its fixtures and fittings sold. The great horn windows, together with the staircase down which Mary Stuart walked to her execution, were sold to William Whitwell, landlord of the Talbot Hotel in Oundle. They still grace this venerable old hostelry and Mary's face is occasionally seen gazing at passers-by from the horn windows.

All that now remains of Fotheringay Castle is the melancholic mound on which it once stood, and where the Scottish thistles that sprout in the summer are poignantly known as 'Queen Mary's tears'.

PREVIOUS PAGES: This misty, melancholic mound is all that survives of Fotheringay Castle, where Mary, Queen of Scots was beheaded.

BELOW: Imagine the author Charles Dickens wandering among these grounds of Rockingham Castle, conjuring up the ghost of one of his own characters.

ROCKINGHAM CASTLE
Nr Market Harborough, Leicestershire Ⓐ
CHARLES DICKENS SEES A GHOST

Built on the orders of William the Conqueror, Rockingham Castle was used by successive Kings of England. It remained a royal castle until the 16th century, when Henry VIII granted it to Edward Watson, whose descendants have lived here ever since. The castle's architecture, while being predominantly Tudor, also boasts sturdy Norman walls. Although the castle's spectral inhabitants are a little thin on the ground, the one reported ghostly sighting is more literary than literal, and tells us more about the man who saw it than it does about any ghosts that may, or may not, walk the corridors at Rockingham Castle.

Charles Dickens (1812–70) was a regular visitor to the castle, being a great friend of the then owners Richard and Lavinia Watson. In November 1849, he spent several days here, and delighted his hosts by acting out scenes from *Nicholas Nickleby* and *School for Scandal* alongside Mrs Watson's cousin, Miss Boyle. The house and grounds certainly wove their magic upon the author's fevered imagination. As 'the first shadows of a new story' began 'hovering in a ghostly way' about him, he made several visits to Rockingham Castle to commit it to memory in preparation for its becoming 'Chesney Wold' in his novel *Bleak House*. Whenever Dickens created a character, the person became very real to him, taking on a life of his or her own. It wasn't unknown for him to hold conversations with his fictitious inventions, and for their fates to affect him in

BELVOIR CASTLE
Belvoir, Leicestershire Ⓐ
A FAMILY OF WITCHES

Belvoir, a name that means 'beautiful view', occupies a commanding position with stunning vistas across the surrounding countryside, and is the ancestral home to the Dukes of Rutland. Francis, 6th Earl of Rutland, lived at Belvoir Castle in the early years of the 17th century. Among the local people employed in his household were a Bottesford woman named Joan Flower and her two daughters, Margaret and Phillipa. They were not a popular family; Joan's neighbours considered her to be 'monstrous and malicious'. She was an ill-kempt woman, with sunken eyes, who boasted of her atheism, consorted with familiar spirits and revelled in the terror that her curses and foul-mouthed oaths instilled in her unfortunate neighbours.

Few people — including the Countess Cecilia, who became increasingly suspicious of them — doubted that the three women were witches. When Margaret Flower was caught pilfering food and other items from the castle, the countess dismissed her on the spot. In so doing, she incurred the wrath of the women who had become known as the Belvoir witches. In concert with the Devil, the three women began casting spells on the earl and his family. Soon afterwards, both Francis and Cecilia became sick, and suffered 'extraordinary convulsions'. Although they recovered, their eldest son, Henry, Lord Roos, was stricken by a sudden illness and died. Then the couple's other son, Francis, Lord Roos, was 'most barbarously and inhumanely tortured by a strange sickness', and he also died. Their daughter, Lady Katherine, was next to feel the smart of the witches' revenge and was 'set upon by their dangerous and devilish practices', although she recovered.

The final straw came when the earl and countess were again 'brought into their snares' to keep them from having any more children. The three women were arrested. While being examined by a Justice of the Peace, Joan Flower called for bread and butter and cried that she wished 'it would never go through' her if she were guilty. Putting the bread into her mouth, she mumbled a few words, and promptly choked to death. Her guilt was affirmed, and with it the fate of her two daughters who were hanged in Lincoln gaol on 11th March 1618. Today, the

sundry ways. Thus it was that, while walking behind the 400-year-old yew hedge during one stay at Rockingham, he is said to have come face-to-face with the ghost of one of the protagonists in *Bleak House*, Lady Dedlock. Since she was a fictional character it is probable that the vision was more hallucinatory than spectral or, as the castle's current owner James Saunders Watson told me; 'Sadly I fear that the story was pure fiction, created by the genius of Charles Dickens'.

TOP: Belvoir Castle, the beautiful home of successive Dukes of Rutland, was once the scene of a series of pitiful tragedies which haunt it still.

OPPOSITE: The tunnel-ridden rocks beneath Nottingham Castle echo with the sound of ghostly pleadings.

effigy of Francis, 6th Earl of Rutland, reclines in the nearby church of St Mary the Virgin, sandwiched between those of his first wife Frances and his second wife Cecilia. His two sons kneel at the foot of the tomb, both holding skulls as symbols of their tragic deaths, whest part of the long-winded inscription recalls how, 'In 1608 he married Lady Cecilia Hungerford… by whom he had two sons, both who died in their infancy by wicked practice and sorcerye…'

NOTTINGHAM CASTLE
Nottingham, Nottinghamshire Ⓐ
THE FRENCH QUEEN
AND THE TRAITOR

Nottingham Castle stands atop an imposing sandstone crag that is riddled with caves and tunnels. One of these is known as 'Mortimer's Hole', named for the man whose ghost is known to haunt it: Roger Mortimer (1287–1330), 1st Earl of March and lover of Queen Isabella, the 'she-wolf of France'. These two infamous characters were a formidable team who instigated the murder of Isabella's husband, Edward II (see page 00) Afterwards Mortimer became king in all but name,

ruling on behalf of the boy Edward III. In October 1330, Mortimer and Isabella arrived at Nottingham Castle to hold a Parliament. Seventeen-year-old Edward had taken lodgings outside the castle, and urged on by his supporters, he determined to rid England of Mortimer's tyranny. On the night of 19th October 1330, Edward and 24 loyal followers entered the labyrinth of secret tunnels that riddle the castle rock. Arriving in the castle itself, they snuck past the guards and burst into Mortimer and Isabella's chamber, where Edward is said to have seized hold of the man responsible for his father's murder. Despite Isabella's pleading, 'Fair son, have mercy on the gentle Mortimer', Edward imprisoned him in the castle, before taking him to London where he had him executed as a traitor. Echoes from that long-ago night are still heard in the modern and un-castle like structure that now occupies the site. In the subterranean chambers where Mortimer was held, footsteps have been heard pacing anxiously back and forth, while from the castle itself a woman's voice is sometimes heard pleading in agitated tones, 'Bel fitz, eiez pitie du gentil Mortimer!'

'BEL FITZ, EIEZ PITIE DU GENTIL MORTIMER!'

ISABELLA PLEADS FOR MORTIMER'S LIFE

LINCOLN CASTLE

Lincoln, Lincolnshire Ⓐ

A GHOSTLY PRESENCE IN THE COFFIN PEWS

Begun in 1068 on the orders of William the Conqueror, Lincoln is one of only two castles in Britain that was built with a double motte. On the larger of the two stands the 15-sided keep known as the Lucy Tower, in commemoration of Lucy, Countess of Chester, mother of Ranulf, Earl of Chester, who was granted permission to refortify the stronghold in the 1140s.

From 1787 to 1878, the castle acted as the city's prison, and it is the Victorian prison chapel that is acknowledged as being the most haunted part. Its coffin-like pews were intended to remind prisoners of the fate awaiting them. Several people have encountered an unseen entity lurking in the tiny-tiered pews, and complain of feeling a cold breeze as an invisible 'something' brushes slowly by them.

TATTERSHALL CASTLE

Tattershall, Lincolnshire Ⓐ

THE GLOWING WHITE LADY

Soaring to a lofty 30.5 metres (100 feet), and comprised of almost one million bricks, the great tower of Tattershall Castle dominates the countryside for far around. It is all that remains of a 15th-century stronghold erected by Ralph Cromwell, Lord Treasurer of England, on the site of an earlier fortification built in 1230 by Robert de Tateshale. Intended as a demonstration of Cromwell's immense power, the tower passed to the Crown when he died without an heir. It was given to the Earls of Lincoln, who allowed the building to fall into decay. In 1910, Lord Curzon intervened to stop sections of the derelict structure being shipped abroad and, having restored it, bequeathed it to the National Trust.

Occasionally, a glimmering White Lady is seen drifting around the battlements when darkness has fallen. Nobody knows for certain who she is, or why she roams the ramparts, although there is a tradition that she is seeking her long-lost love. It is possible that she is the same woman who appears inside the building from time to time, wearing a white gown with a Norman headdress. Whether she is also the night-time prankster who sometimes scatters leaflets around a turret room in an apparent fit of phantom pique is unknown.

ABOVE: Lincoln Castle began life in the 11th century as a traditional defence atop an unusual double motte; its chilling 'presence' dates from when a prison chapel was added in Victorian times.

OPPOSITE: The 15th-century Tattershall Castle's grandiose exterior is rather diminished by the antics of a phantom prankster who visits during the hours of darkness.

TORTURED LOVERS, VENGEFUL SISTERS and SINISTER SHADES

There is a silence where hath been no sound,
There is a silence where no sound may be,
In the cold grave – under the deep, deep sea,
Or in wide desert where no life is found;
Which hath been mute, and still must sleep profound;

FROM *SILENCE*
BY THOMAS HOOD (1799–1845)

SHROPSHIRE, STAFFORDSHIRE, DERBYSHIRE & MERSEYSIDE

These counties offer an intriguing contrast of beautiful scenery and industrial landscapes. The coal, iron and other mineral deposits that were found here helped fuel the expansion of the British Empire and have left visible scars all across the region.

Within this industrial heartland, however, one also finds the awesome beauty of the Peak District. Here, bleak moorland is broken by rocky tors, crags and gorges, and underground caverns conceal dark watercourses and magical arrays of stalactites and stalagmites.

Meanwhile, tranquil pastures and hills in Shropshire belie the area's turbulent past. The border with Wales placed the county in the vanguard of the English force against the threat of a Welsh uprising. The inhabitants of Shropshire had to keep a constant eye on the distant mountains, and be ever vigilant for signs of an invasion.

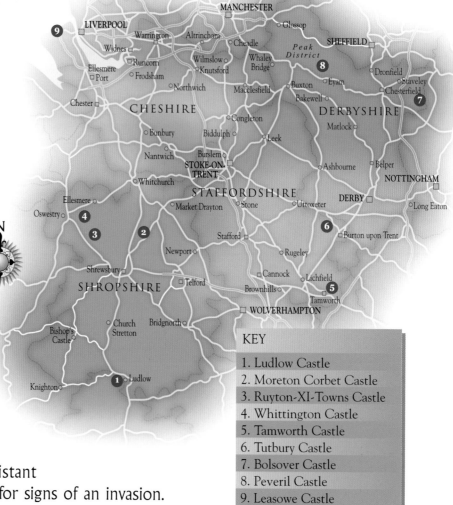

KEY

1. Ludlow Castle
2. Moreton Corbet Castle
3. Ruyton-XI-Towns Castle
4. Whittington Castle
5. Tamworth Castle
6. Tutbury Castle
7. Bolsover Castle
8. Peveril Castle
9. Leasowe Castle

An aura of departed greatness hangs over the region's castles, many of which dominate their surroundings. They gaze down from their rocky thrones, their shattered walls reflecting past eras of grandeur and mystery. Their ghosts belong to all ages, and transcend the centuries, commemorating deeds that were sometimes brave, other times infamous, occasionally mysterious, but always thrilling.

LUDLOW CASTLE
Ludlow, Shropshire Ⓐ
LOVE AND BETRAYAL IN THE MARSHES

It was to Ludlow Castle that Henry VII sent his eldest son Arthur to act as his Regent in Wales. In 1502, the prince took his young Spanish bride, Catherine of Aragon there, and established an alternative court, modelled on the one at Westminster. A few months later, Arthur died, and his wife wept beside the body of the boy to whom she had been married for barely six months. She would later wed his brother Henry in a union that was destined to bring cataclysmic change to England. There are few British castles that present the visitor with such a great feeling of 'What if?' as Ludlow. Standing in the roofless suite of rooms where Arthur died, you can't help pondering how different things might have been had he lived and had Catherine borne him sons. His brother, rather than becoming King Henry VIII, would have been Archbishop of Canterbury. There would have been no Church of England, no Reformation and no Elizabeth I.

However, speculation is redundant, for die he did and, with his death, Ludlow ceased to be a royal court. The ghost of Ludlow Castle belongs to an earlier period in the history of this much-disputed borderland between England and Wales. Powerful and self-seeking Lords of the Marches – each of whom was virtually an independent monarch behind the walls of his castle – guarded the border with Wales. From strongholds such as Ludlow, they kept a wary watch on the distant hills, lest a darting shadow might signal the start of a Welsh uprising.

In the reign of Henry I (1068–1135), Ludlow Castle was owned by the Marcher lord, Josse de Dinant, who fought a perpetual struggle to hold Ludlow against both the Welsh and two powerful fellow nobles, Hugh Mortimer and Walter de Lacy. One day, Josse had the good fortune to capture Mortimer. Having imprisoned him in a tower that still bears his name he was able to extract a hefty ransom from his family for his release. A few years later, following a pitched battle, the Lord of Ludlow managed to capture de Lacy and two of his knights, all of whom were incarcerated in Ludlow's Pendover

ABOVE: Ludlow Castle was where Prince Arthur, the first husband of Catherine of Aragon, died in 1502; his death changed the course of English history.

PREVIOUS PAGES: Derbyshire's 17th-century Bolsover Castle sometimes rings with the chilling sound of a wailing baby.

LEFT: The strange feeling of unease that emanates from the walls of Moreton Corbet Castle date from its rebuilding in the early 17th century.

BELOW: The ghostly mist that sometimes engulfs Ruyton-XI-Towns Castle will set your nerves jangling and your teeth chattering.

Tower. However, the three prisoners escaped in time-honoured fashion by way of a rope of knotted linen, thoughtfully provided by a castle beauty, Marion de la Bruyère, who had fallen in love with one of their number, Arnold de Lys.

Later, Josse set out on a journey and left his castle without a lord. Marion, who was still besotted with Arnold, sent word that she was almost alone in the castle and, if he cared to visit her, she would open a window and fling down a rope. Arnold told his friend de Lacy of her offer, and the two agreed that this was the perfect opportunity for a decidedly dastardly deed. Thus it was that Arnold stealthily climbed the rope and

was soon embroiled in a passionate embrace with the unsuspecting Marion. Meanwhile, in the darkness outside, 100 of de Lacy's men ascended the rope and snuck into the castle, where they slew the watchman and opened the gates. As the main force charged in and proceeded to slaughter the garrison, Marion realized that she had been sorely used. Leaping from her lover's arms, she grabbed his sword and, having run him through, let out a howl of indignant despair, leapt from the window and died on the rocks below.

Returning from his journey, Josse laid siege to the castle, but despite burning down the huge outer door, was unable to retake it. Meanwhile de Lacy committed an almighty breach of border etiquette, and called upon the Welsh for support. Led by the Princes of Gwynedd and Powys, Welsh reinforcements

'THY HOUSE SHALL
BE FULL OF DOLEFUL
CREATURES.'

HOLMYARD CURSES HIS FORMER HOST

came streaming over the border, captured Josse and locked him up in his own castle. When Henry I heard what had happened, he was furious and ordered de Lacy to release his captive and send the Welsh home. The first command was obeyed immediately. But it took four years of bribery, negotiation and fighting to drive the Welsh from the Shropshire Marches.

The castle now stands in ruins, a hollow shell alone with its memories. But from time to time the anguished wails of Marion de la Bruyère echo down the centuries to shatter the silence of the night hours. Occasionally, the wispy white form of her sorrowful wraith is also seen, a trapped spirit doomed to linger at the site of her betrayal, and condemned to re-enact her fatal plunge over and over again.

MORETON CORBET CASTLE
Moreton Corbet, Shropshire Ⓡ Ⓔ
THE PURITAN'S CURSE

Walking among the hollow ruins of the castle and unfinished Elizabethan mansion can be an unnerving experience. Your footsteps echo; shadows dance around you; and there is the constant feeling that you are not alone. It is, without doubt, a chilling place, over which wash ripples of fear and fascination in equal proportions.

Sir Robert Corbet began to build the house on the site of the earlier castle in 1606. Before he was able to finish it, he died of plague in London and his brother, Vincent, inherited the property. It was a time when James I was persecuting the Puritans, although Sir Vincent, unlike many of his peers, was a

tolerant landlord who at first gladly gave refuge to an outspoken Puritan, Paul Holmyard. When Holmyard's ideals became more extreme, and his outbursts more vociferous, Vincent Corbet asked him to leave. Holmyard survived for a time in the nearby woods, but was then captured and taken to Shrewsbury Gaol. Not before he had confronted his erstwhile protector, however. Corbet was surveying the foundations of his home when the captured Puritan passed by. Holmyard spat a curse at Corbet. 'Woe unto thee, man of the hardened heart,' he snarled, 'hardened even as the Lord hardened the heart of Pharaoh, to thy own destruction. Rejoice not in thy wealth, nor in the halls of thy pride; for there shall never be a copestone set upon them, neither shalt thou, nor thy children, nor thy children's children, dwell therein; but they shall be a ruin and a desolation, and the snake and the eft and the adder shall be found there, and thy house shall be full of doleful creatures.'

True to the prophecy, the house was never finished. Later members of the family decided to build elsewhere, and abandoned Moreton Corbet Castle to the ravages of time. The bedraggled ghost of Paul Holmyard is said to stalk the hollow ruins to ensure that no building work is ever done.

RUYTON-XI-TOWNS CASTLE
Ruyton-XI-Towns, Shropshire Ⓡ
PHANTOM HORSEMAN RIDES THE ROLLING MIST

The curious name of this red-sandstone village came about when 11 small hamlets were united in 1301. As a result, its main street stretches for 1.6 kilometres (1 mile) and is one of the

longest in the country. Its most eye-catching landmark is the massive battlemented tower of the church, next to which are located the remnants of the 14th-century castle. Explore the ruins on a halcyon summer's day, when a gentle breeze wafts the pastoral scent of wild flowers around the site, and you can feel centuries removed from the stresses and pressures of the modern age. But return here in the dead of night, and a terrifying encounter might well await you. It will start with a mist that gathers in the valley before rolling towards the church and castle, its density increasing into a thick, swirling miasma. You become disorientated and hear the whinnying of a horse, followed by the fog-dulled thudding of its hooves galloping towards you. Suddenly the mist parts, and the hideous sight of a headless horseman springs from the murky vapour and heads towards the castle keep. A cold chill sets your teeth chattering as you watch him melt into the stonework and, as he disappears, the mist recedes. Then, like

many before, you will feel as though you have woken from a hazy dream, and may well turn heel and run, determined to escape whatever other surprises the night might have in store.

WHITTINGTON CASTLE
Whittington, Shropshire ®
THE CURSED CHEST

The charming village of Whittington, with its quaintly archaic houses and rustic pubs, possesses the ambience of a bygone age. Its centrepiece is undoubtedly the romantic and strikingly beautiful ruin of Whittington Castle, which dates from the 12th century and is currently the subject of a unique experiment. In 1998, the villagers, concerned about their castle's future, formed a charitable trust to purchase the site and preserve it for the enjoyment and benefit of future generations. Thanks to their dedication, the castle's future is now assured, and it is possible to make your way to this peaceful, unspoilt part of rural Shropshire to immerse yourself in the legends and history of a truly magical place.

William Peverel built the Norman motte-and-bailey castle. As he had no sons, his eldest daughter, Mellet, was destined to inherit the estate. To ensure that she married a man who would be worthy of such an heirloom, Peverel ordered that a great tournament be held. The victor would win his daughter's hand, along with ownership of the castle. Warin de Metz of Lorraine beat off fierce competition to take the prize, and became the founding father of a dynasty of Fitzwarines that held the castle for several centuries. In 1222, the family rebuilt it in stone, and much of what survives today dates from this period.

Only two of its original seven magnificent towers survive. Yet these two graceful towers, whose pale images flicker in the tranquil waters of the moat, possess a haunted feel, and occasionally the sorrowful faces of two ghostly children have been seen, peering from the tiny slit windows. No one knows their identity, but there is a general consensus that they may be linked to one of the castle's more chilling and enigmatic furnishings – the cursed chest.

This impressive Elizabethan casket, weighing a hefty half tonne (10cwt), is of unknown origin. It has long been rumoured that should the casket ever be opened, the heir to the Whittington estate will die in agony. It is suggested that the childish shades might be long-ago heirs who had the misfortune to live at a time when the true virulence of the curse was unrealized. Certainly no one in recent centuries has dared unleash whatever malevolent force is lurking within the chest. Such is its fearsome reputation, that it was kept hidden away for many years, the key thrown into he moat to prevent a chance opening. Recently it was removed from the castle, ostensibly for safe keeping!

ABOVE: The Norman tower of Tamworth Castle was where a nobleman encountered a long-dead abbess bent on vengeance for the desecration of her convent.

OPPOSITE: Look carefully at the high windows of Whittington's beautiful castle – you may see the sorrowful faces of two ghostly children.

TAMWORTH CASTLE
Tamworth, Staffordshire Ⓐ
THE ADMONISHING SISTER OF LITTLE MERCY

Tamworth Castle was begun just after the Norman Conquest, and later became the property of royal champion Robert de Marmion, who is said to have expelled the nuns from the nearby convent at Polesworth. This act had incurred the spectral displeasure of St Editha, its long-dead founder. She appeared one night at his bedside and threatened him with a violent and untimely death if he didn't allow the nuns to return to their rightful home. To emphasize the point, she smote him across the head with her crozier, causing blood to flow from the resultant wound. The admonishing apparition so terrified de Marmion that he quickly restored the confiscated lands to the nuns. The middle room of the Norman tower is where the Baron de Marmion reputedly met with the fearful sister of little mercy and, in commemoration of the ghastly occurrence, it is today known as the 'ghost room'. The spectral nun has appeared to several startled witnesses here and, on account of the colour of her habit, is known as the Black Lady of Tamworth.

Whether it is she who is behind the strange phenomenon that plagues other parts of the castle is uncertain. A custodian who was one morning opening the former bedrooms that have now been converted into an exhibition called the 'Tamworth Story', was temporarily blinded when what felt like sand was flung into her face. Recovering, she looked down expecting to see her clothes covered in grit, but found nothing. Looking up she saw a mass of smoke, about 2 metres (6 feet) high, moving towards the window where it suddenly vanished.

At around 11.30pm on 24th February 1999, the police contacted a castle key holder to tell her that the building's alarms had gone off, but a thorough search of the premises revealed no sign of a break-in. The lady phoned the alarm company, who promised to send an engineer round. As she awaited his arrival, she heard footsteps in the room above, followed by the sound of a heavy table being dragged across the floor. This went on for the best part of an hour. When the engineer arrived, the custodian went to let him in and he expressed surprise at how quickly she had reached him. Asked to elaborate, he explained that he had seen a lady waving to him from the window of the upstairs room, from which the mysterious sounds had been emanating.

TUTBURY CASTLE
Tutbury, Staffordshire Ⓐ
ENIGMATIC WHITE LADY

Tutbury Castle was originally built in 1071 but was destroyed in 1174 when its then owner, William Ferrers, rebelled against King Henry II. When it was rebuilt, Henry III gave the castle to his younger son Edmund who, in 1267, was created Earl of Lancaster. It has remained in the hands of the Dukes and Earls of Lancaster ever since. In 1362, John of Gaunt, second Duke of Lancaster, obtained permission to repair the castle, and over the next century, it was rebuilt and extended.

Tutbury's most famous resident was undoubtedly Mary, Queen of Scots, who was imprisoned there from 1569–70 and again from 1585–86. She found its hilltop location extremely uncomfortable, and afterwards maintained that her true imprisonment had only began when she was brought to Tutbury. Mary described the castle as sitting squarely on top of a mountain at the centre of a plain and entirely exposed to all the winds and 'injures' of heaven. The malodorous fumes that wafted up from the marsh below offended her delicate sensibilities, whilst her health suffered from the constant damp and ceaseless draughts. Having experienced so much misery at Tutbury Castle,

Mary — whose spirit must be one of the busiest in Britain — may well have returned several times to haunt the place that she held in such low esteem. Some believe that she is the ghostly white lady whose sombre form has been known to glide around the watchtower, leaving a cold chill and astonished witnesses in her wake. Others, however, maintain that this particular revenant is, in fact, that of a former mistress of the castle who embarked upon a passionate affair. One night, having arrived at the tower for an illicit assignation, she was horrified to discover her lover lying dead in a pool of blood. Turning, she found the castle steward standing behind her, a bloodied sword in his hand. Letting out a howl of anguished despair, the heartbroken mistress rushed forward and impaled herself upon the deadly blade. And it is her ghost, some say, that has remained at the place of her demise ever since. Whoever this enigmatic White Lady was in life, in death she has chilled the marrow of many a visitor by fixing them with a malicious stare.

White ladies of uncertain identity aside, several other past residents of the castle return in spirit form. Among them is the apparition of an old woman, whose phantom has floated before many a visitor in the vicinity of the great hall. At other locations, a ghostly child has been known to run past startled witnesses and even, on occasion, to touch them with an icy hand. The King's Bedchamber is another of the castle's haunted rooms, where orbs of light have frequently been seen hovering in mid air, and several people have experienced the alarming sensation of having their hands held by an invisible, clammy form. Finally there is the ghostly tattoo sounded by an unseen drummer and which is most often heard around the castle's North Tower. Many visitors who do not actually see the ghosts of Tutbury complain of feeling uneasy as they explore the ruins.

BOLSOVER CASTLE
Bolsover, Derbyshire Ⓐ Ⓔ
THE SPECTRAL INFANT'S GHASTLY CRIES

The present Bolsover Castle dates from the 17th century, when Charles Cavendish demolished the old stronghold that had been built in the 12th century by William Peveril, and replaced

OPPOSITE TOP: Mary, Queen of Scots, who insisted that her first true prison was Tutbury Castle. She was confined there on two occasions, in 1569 and 1585.

OPPOSITE BOTTOM: Little now remains of Tutbury Castle, where Mary, Queen of Scots complained of the draught and several ghosts join her on nebulous strolls.

RIGHT: The bulk of Bolsover Castle rises high above the surrounding Derbyshire woodland, but it is in the 'Little Castle', with its Jacobean panelling and fireplaces, that are haunted by a young woman and her baby.

it with a functional family home. Consequently, very little now survives of the original Norman fortress, but what does is subject to a plethora of strange phenomena. Phantom smells and spectral slaps are just a few of the experiences to which bemused visitors have been subjected. None is more chilling than the apparition of a young woman who has been seen striding into the kitchens of the so-called 'Little Castle'. She wears a look of fearful apprehension, as if she is being pursued, and carries a bundle under her arm. Suddenly, she opens the oven doors and throws the bundle in, whereupon a baby's screams are heard. As the cries fade away, so too does the ghostly woman, leaving behind troubled witnesses, several of whom have vowed never to set foot in the castle again.

PEVERIL CASTLE
Castleton, Derbyshire Ⓐ Ⓔ
SOOTHING SOUND OF SINGING LADY

Known as the 'castle of the peak' and occupying a virtually impregnable position on its rocky, windswept platform, the dramatic ruin of Peveril Castle dates from the late 11th century and is named for William Peveril, an illegitimate son of William the Conqueror. There was a time when local people would climb to the top of Castle Hill at 6am on Easter Sunday as, 'on this day the sun is said to dance for joy at his rising'. But such customs are now a thing of the past, and today the castle's chief claim to fame is that Sir Walter Scott immortalized it in his novel *Peveril of the Peak*.

There is a certain 'other-worldliness' about the majestic ruin, and many who visit it claim to find it imbued with a strange, indefinable aura of unease. Some claim to have seen the shade of a white knight standing near the ramparts, while a phantom dog and ghostly horse have also been seen in the vicinity of the ruined keep. Occasionally, when soaring clouds have cast long shadows over the castle, people have also been alarmed by the sound of an ethereal lady singing a soft lament from the sombre ruins.

LEASOWE CASTLE
Moreton, Merseyside 🛏
THE GHOSTLY COMPANY OF FATHER AND SON

The sea-sprayed façade of Leasowe Castle presents an intriguing mishmash of different architectural styles. Part castellated stronghold, part black-and-white timber-framed house, it is now a delightful hotel where guests can enjoy copious quantities of the bracing sea air that swirls around its ancient walls. Built in 1593, the castle was originally the summer home of Ferdinando, the 5th Lord Derby. However, within a century of construction, the family seem to have tired of it and allowed it to fall into ruin. Such was its state of neglect that by 1680 it was known as 'Mockbeggar Hall', a name given to old and ruinous manorial houses. Since then it has seen use as a private home, a hostel for sailors and a convalescent home for railway workers, before metamorphosing into the magnificent hotel that it is today.

No matter what its use, or who its owners, there are two residents who have remained here for centuries, and whose night-time wanderings have become legendary. They are a man and boy, supposedly father and son, who at some stage in the castle's past, were captured in the course of an ancient family feud and taken there as prisoners. Tradition makes no mention of when this bitter quarrel erupted, but only states that father and son were imprisoned in the castle's oak room while the owners decided what to do with them. Realizing that their decision would no doubt bode ill for them both, the father, fearful of the torture their captors might inflict upon the boy, suffocated him with a pillow. The dreadful deed done, he proceeded to dash out his own brains by banging his head furiously against the wall until he too fell dead.

When the castle first opened its doors to paying guests in the 19th century, this chamber was used as one of the bedrooms. Many guests would wake in the early hours of the morning to find the glowing forms of the phantom father and son standing by the window. Although reports of their haunting continue, it has been observed that their forlorn figures are returning less and less, and that whenever they do they are somehow less distinct. Perhaps the horror of their final moments is weakening, and the day is at hand when their nebulous perambulations will be nothing more than just one of the many memories to which such a venerable property is inevitably a silent guardian.

LEFT: Leasowe's architectural style has suffered from several additions over the centuries, but its spectral residents are constant.

OPPOSITE: When cloud shadows fall over the ruins of Peveril Castle, the melodious lament of a lady is heard.

BROODING GUARDIANS *of* FORGOTTEN SECRETS

We are not sure of sorrow,
And joy was never sure;
To-day will die to-morrow;
Time stoops to no man's lure;
And love, grown faint and fretful,
With lips but half regretful
Sighs, and with eyes forgetful
Weeps that no loves endure.

FROM *THE GARDEN OF PROSERPINE*
BY ALGERNON CHARLES SWINBURNE (1837–1909)

WALES

Wales is often called the 'Land of Castles', and it is home to some of Europe's finest and most imposing medieval strongholds. The most impressive are undoubtedly those that resulted from Edward I's decision in 1276 to treat the Welsh princes as insurgents. He aimed for an outright conquest, and built series of strategically linked fortresses from which he could subdue the territory once and for all. Thus began one of the biggest programmes of castle-building ever inaugurated by an English monarch. The massive bastions were intended to frighten the native Welsh into submission, end their hopes of nationalism forever, and provide them with a permanent reminder of their true ruler. Many of them are as impressive today as in the past, and the ghosts that roam among them testify to both the virulence of the times in which they were built and to the centuries of unrest which they have since witnessed.

KEY

1. Raglan Castle
2. Caerphilly Castle
3. Ogmore Castle
4. Pennard Castle
5. Kidwelly Castle
6. Carew Castle
7. Roch Castle
8. Powis Castle
9. Ewloe Castle
10. Ruthin Castle
11. Denbigh Castle
12. Rhuddlan Castle
13. Caernarfon Castle

RAGLAN CASTLE
Raglan, Monmouthshire Ⓐ
THE BOOKISH BOGIE

Towering majestically over its surrounding landscape, this imposing ruin was the last true castle built in the whole of England and Wales. Begun in around 1432 by Sir William ap Thomas, it was eulogized by the 15th-century poet Dafydd Llwyd for its 'hundred rooms filled with festive fare, its hundred towers, parlours and doors, its hundred heaped-up fires of long dried fuel' and 'its hundred chimneys for men of high degree'. In 1492, it passed into the possession of the Somerset family, the powerful Earls of Worcester. Successive generations of Worcesters continued to expand and enhance the castle, until, by the 17th century, it had become a rambling though impressive bastion, the ruins of

which are still awe-inspiring. During the English Civil War, Raglan was held by Henry Somerset, a Royalist of such staunchness that he contributed almost £1,000,000 to the royal cause, and entertained the ill-fated Charles I at Raglan on more than one occasion. Besieged by the Parliamentarians, the garrison held out for a remarkable three months before Henry Somerset surrendered Raglan Castle to his adversaries on 19th August 1646. As General Fairfax and his officers entered the outward court, Raglan's days of glory drew to a close. Unappreciated by the victors, it was stripped of its timbers and fittings and abandoned to the elements, never to be lived in again.

Today, a soothing atmosphere permeates the rambling interior of the old ruin. Some visitors have been startled by fleeting glimpses of what they describe as a 'bardic' figure, beckoning to them from the vicinity of the wing over which the library was once situated. He is thought to be the ghost of the castle's librarian who, as the Civil War siege ebbed towards its inevitable conclusion, hid the valuable books and manuscripts in a secret tunnel beneath the castle. His fears proved well founded, for one of the first acts perpetrated by the enemy was the destruction of Raglan's magnificent and priceless library. The fate of the librarian is unknown, but his guardian spirit still watches over his hidden cache of literary treasures. He was last seen in the summer of 2001, when a girl on a school trip came running from the castle, ashen-faced, insisting that she had seen him

ABOVE: In its day, Raglan Castle served as both palace and fortress, and its resident ghost is a librarian who suffered an unknown fate in England's Civil War in the 17th century.

RIGHT: The impressive water defences that surround Caerphilly Castle are no guard against the ghost of a broken-hearted green lady.

PREVIOUS PAGES: Exposed to whipping, sand- and salt-laden sea winds, the desolate ruins of Pennard Castle are a place where insanity reigns at night.

gesturing to her from a dimly lit corner. Bookish bogies aside, there is no denying that Raglan Castle possesses a mysterious aura, and no one who treads its gloom-laden passageways and dark, twisting stairwells, or gazes upon its huge hollow windows, can deny that a certain spine-tingling strangeness hangs over the entire foundation.

CAERPHILLY CASTLE
Caerphilly, Glamorgan Ⓐ
GREEN FOR JEALOUSY

The massive bulk of Caerphilly Castle, surrounded by sprawling and impressive water defences, is not only the largest castle in Wales but is also one of Europe's greatest medieval strongholds. Constructed between 1268 and 1271, it stands as a proud testimony to its original owner and builder, Red Gilbert de Clare (1263–95), so-called because of the flaming colour of his hair, which was matched by his tempestuous and fiery nature.

He was married to the beautiful princess, Alice of Angouleme, a lady of refined tastes and passionate nature, who came to resent her husband's warring disposition. One day, Gruffudd the Fair, Prince of Brithdir, paid a visit to the castle. Alice became enamoured with this handsome and amorous Welsh prince, and soon the two were lovers. Rather

enriching experience. A man living nearby once woke in the middle of the night to find her apparition hovering, uninvited, at his bedside. She motioned him to follow her and, despite considerable reservations, he felt strangely compelled to do so.

The lady led him to the moonlit ruins of Ogmore Castle and bade him lift a certain stone. He obeyed, and beneath the stone, he found a cauldron brimming with gold coins.

'Take half for yourself and replace the stone over the rest,' she told him. Eagerly, the man filled his pockets and replaced the stone over the treasure. He looked up to thank his ghostly benefactor, but she had disappeared. Nevertheless, it was as a wealthy man that he left Ogmore Castle that night. His newfound status soon became the talk of the neighbourhood, but he steadfastly refused to reveal the source of his riches.

Despite now possessing sufficient wealth to live in luxury for the rest of his days, his thoughts kept turning to the remaining coins. One night his greed got the better of him, and returning to the castle he located the stone and raised it. There were the gold coins glinting in the moonlight. But no sooner had he begun to fill his pockets than a cold chill ran down his spine. Looking up, he saw the White Lady gazing at him, shaking her head in admonishment. 'Foolish man,' she chided. 'You have all you could ever need, and yet you still want more. From this night forth your fortunes shall be reversed.' Moments later she was gone.

The man hastily replaced gold and the stone and hurried home. In the weeks that followed, he became ill, and despite the best medical attention – which he could well afford – his condition worsened. He did finally reveal the source of his wealth and confess his folly, but took the secret of the cauldron's exact location to the grave. Although many have sought it since, none have ever found it.

foolishly, Gruffudd confessed their secret to a monk who turned out to be duplicitous and informed the cuckolded husband. A deranged Gilbert sent his wife back to France and ordered his men to find Gruffudd. Learning of the friar's betrayal, Gruffudd caught the monk and hanged him from a tree at a site now known as 'Monk's Vale' in commemoration. No sooner had he done so than Gilbert's men caught up with him, and he too was soon dangling at the end of a noose.

Gleefully, the avenged husband sent a messenger to France to inform Alice of her lover's execution. Such was the shock of the news that she dropped dead on the spot and her ghost has haunted the ramparts of Caerphilly Castle ever since. Resplendent in a richly woven dress, coloured green for Gilbert's envy, she waits in silent solitude, desperate to be reunited with her princely lover whose flattering attentions fate has long denied her.

OGMORE CASTLE
Ogmore, Vale of Glamorgan ®
THE BOUNTIFUL WHITE LADY

Peacefully situated on the lush banks of the River Ewenny, the meagre remains of Ogmore Castle hark back to the days when the Normans held their Welsh estates by the power of their swords. Begun in the early 12th century by William de Londres, it guarded a major fording place into southern Wales. Although its history is fairly uneventful, it possesses a serene and enchanting aura, with the added bonus that a chance encounter with its ghostly White Lady could prove a truly

ABOVE: The benign setting of Ogmore Castle has hidden dangers: its White Lady could make you very wealthy, but misfortune will strike if you abuse her largesse.

OPPOSITE: Kidwelly Castle was sometimes in Welsh hands, sometimes in English – so its ghostly sentry could be of either nationality.

PENNARD CASTLE
Nr Southgate, Glamorgan ℞
THE FAIRY CURSE AND THE FEARSOME PHANTOM

Perched upon its rocky throne overlooking the beautiful Three Cliffs Bay, Pennard Castle is as picturesque a ruin as you could ever wish to find. Originally constructed in the 12th century by Henry de Beaumont, 1st Earl of Warwick, and rebuilt in the late 13th and early 14th centuries by the de Broase family, little is known of the castle's history and it would appear that no noteworthy historical events ever took place here. A small settlement developed around the fortress, but by the middle of the 15th century, sand blow had virtually overwhelmed the entire site and both village and castle were abandoned. But where history remains mute, legend swirls in abundance, and thus this dramatic site is, reputedly, both haunted and cursed.

A powerful chieftain is said to have once resided at Pennard. Having one day won a great battle, he was rewarded with the hand of the Welsh ruler's daughter in marriage. Flushed by his success, this bold warrior held a celebratory feast, but in the midst of the proceedings, a worried sentry reported seeing strange lights in the valley below. The furious chieftain grabbed his sword, ordered his army to follow, and marched from the castle to bestow summary justice on those who had dared interrupt his merrymaking. What they found was a group of fairies enjoying a party of their own, dancing around glimmering moonbeams. The chieftain and his men raced at the fairies, swords drawn, hacking and stabbing and thrusting, but the little people proved impervious to their weapons. Their leader turned on their attackers: 'Stop thy warring ways. Spears or swords cannot harm us. Cursed shall you and your castle be, for spoiling our innocent games.' With that the fairies vanished and a great storm suddenly erupted, lifting the sands in a frenzied whirlwind that overcame the chief and his army and then howled inland to engulf Pennard Castle.

The fortress was reduced to the mouldering ruin that can be seen today, believed to be the haunt of a *gwrach-y-rhibyn* — a phantom not unlike the Irish banshee. She is said to roam the castle grounds, in search of the exceedingly brave, or decidedly foolish, who dare spend the night among the enigmatic ruins. Should she encounter such a person, she will let loose a howl of spectral rage and her unfortunate victim will be rendered instantly insane.

> ## 'CURSED SHALL YOU AND YOUR CASTLE BE, FOR SPOILING OUR INNOCENT GAMES.'
>
> LEADER OF THE FAIRIES TO THE CHIEFTAIN OF PENNARD CASTLE

KIDWELLY CASTLE
Kidwelly, Carmarthenshire Ⓐ
THE GLOWERING SENTRY

On every count Kidwelly is an impressive castle. Its sprawling mass of grey stone stands proud and defiant upon its rocky throne, overlooking a tranquil stretch of the River Gwendraeth. Founded in the reign of Henry I (1100–35) it has enjoyed a chequered history, and in its early years, ownership fluctuated between the Normans and the Welsh, reflecting the unsettledness of the times. Today, the magnificent and

substantial remains inspire fear and wonder in equal proportions. As you approach the squat and forbidding gatehouse, the walls of which are punctured by dark slit windows, an indefinable feeling of chilling unease descends upon you. Wandering the dark and eerie interior, you get the distinct feeling that you are being watched, and it comes as little surprise to learn that several visitors have encountered the looming form of a spectral medieval sentry, who stands glowering at them from the darker recesses of the gatehouse.

CAREW CASTLE
Carew, nr Tenby, Pembrokeshire Ⓐ
A GHOSTLY DOMAIN

In 1100, Gerald of Windsor married the beautiful Princess Nest and built the first castle on this site, which he had acquired as part of his wife's dowry. Nest was the greatest beauty of her age, and was nicknamed 'the Helen of Wales'. By the time of her marriage she had already acquired a royal lover in the robust shape of Prince Henry, later to become King Henry I, by whom she had the first of her many offspring. She had five legitimate children with Gerald before, nine years after their marriage, Owain ap Cadwgan, a prince of Ceredigion, and her distant cousin, became enraptured by her beauty and stormed the castle, determined to carry her off. Tradition holds that when she heard her would-be kidnapper banging on their bedroom door, she urged her husband to escape down the toilet shaft, and then allowed herself to be carried away to her cousin's

Ceredigion love nest. Following the intervention of King Henry I, who threatened Owain with terrible reprisals, Nest eventually returned to Carew Castle, though not before she had borne Owain two children. A few years later, Gerald avenged his degradation by killing Owain in an ambush.

When Gerald died in 1116, Nest married Stephen, castellan of Cardigan, by whom she had several more children. Following her death her spirit remained earthbound as a 'White Lady', whose shimmering form would drift through the corridors, passageways and stairwells of the subsequent castles that sprang up on the site.

In the 17th century, the reclusive Sir Roland Rhys took up the tenancy of the castle and secreted himself away in the North-west Tower, where his favourite companion was a pet ape, brought from the Barbary Coast of Africa. One day, his son eloped with the daughter of a local Flemish merchant whose name was Horwitz. The girl's father was livid, and turned up at the castle to confront Sir Roland. Following a heated exchange, Sir Roland set his ape upon the outraged man. The beast administered a savage mauling from which the wretched Horowitz only just managed to escape. As he fled, he cursed Sir Roland and wished the same fate upon him. That night the stillness of the early hours was shattered by terrible screams sounding from the tower. The servants rushed to investigate and found their master lying dead in a pool of blood, his throat ripped open, and his corpse surrounded by the carnage of blood-spattered furniture and torn tapestries. The ape, which had evidently turned against his owner in fulfilment of Horowitz's curse, also lay dead. But on certain evenings the ape's ghost is said to mount the stairway and climb to the battlements of the North-west Tower, from where it emits a loud howl that echoes through the night and rebounds around the ivy-clad walls of this intriguing and atmospheric monument.

ROCH CASTLE
Nr Haverfordwest, Pembrokeshire Ⓢ

SHADE OF A LOYAL ROYAL MISTRESS

In the early 1300s, a witch prophesied that Adam de Rupe would die from the venomous bite of a serpent or adder unless he was able to avoid their fatal sting for a period of one year. Should he do so, he had nothing more to fear and would go on to live a long and happy life. Determined to survive, he built Roch Castle atop an isolated, rocky outcrop and, having moved in to its highest storey, prepared to stay put for the next twelve months. His day-to-day existence was mundane, but de Rupe was consoled

OPPOSITE: The splendid Carew Castle is shared by a conventional ghostly white lady and a decidedly unconventional Barbary ape!

by the fact that no slithering agent of death would be able to get anywhere near him. Finally, the day of his release from the prophecy drew near, but then a particularly harsh spell of wintry weather settled upon the land, and icy winds turned de Rupe's flesh blue and set his teeth chattering. He ordered his manservant to fetch some wood so that a roaring fire might warm the last days of his confinement. Unfortunately, a snake had concealed itself among the logs and, as de Rupe stoked the fire, it reared up and sank its fangs into him. And so the prophecy was fulfilled.

After such dramatic beginnings, the castle's subsequent history was relatively uneventful. The de Rupe family died out in 1420 and their stronghold passed through several owners until coming into the possession of the Walter family in the mid-17th century. During the Civil War, the castle was garrisoned by the Royalists, and saw much action. In 1644, it was captured by the Parliamentarians, then retaken by

ABOVE: Lucy Walter, the mistress of Charles II, still walks Roch Castle, the place of her birth.

BELOW: Roch Castle was erected on the top of a rocky outcrop, to be beyond the reach of the snakes that were, with good reason, feared by its first owner.

the Royalists, before falling once more to Cromwell's forces. Lucy Walter, who was born at Roch Castle in 1630, demonstrated her Royalist sympathies by becoming the mistress of Charles II. She bore him a son, James, whom Charles made Duke of Monmouth and who would grow up to become the ill-fated leader of the 1685 Monmouth Rebellion and end his days on the headsman's block. Perhaps it is the fate of her son that brings Lucy Walter back to Roch Castle where, garbed in a white dress, she passes effortlessly through locked doors.

POWIS CASTLE
Nr Welshpool, Powys Ⓐ 🏵
THE SPINSTER AND THE SPECTRE

In 1780, an elderly spinster arrived at the soaring red sandstone walls of Powis Castle, where she hoped to earn a little money spinning hemp and flax for the household. The earl and his family were away in London, but the steward and small detachment of servants seemed more than happy to give the old lady employment, and even offered her a free night's accommodation. What the poor woman did not realize was that they intended to enjoy a little spooky sport at her expense, by putting her in a bedroom that was known to be haunted. As the door closed behind them, she was a little perturbed to hear it being locked from the outside. Any fears she may have had were soon dispelled by the sheer opulence of the room and, reasoning that they probably did not want a stranger wandering the castle at night, the woman sat by the fire, and began reading her bible.

Moments later she heard the door open and, turning round, saw a man in a gold-laced suit enter the room and cross to the window, where he proceeded to gaze out into the night. A little time later he turned and, without uttering a word, left the room. Something about her mysterious visitor convinced the woman that he was not of this world and, kneeling down, she begged God to protect her. Suddenly, the door opened again and the stranger drifted silently back into the room. This time, emboldened by her prayers, the spinster confronted the phantom. 'Who are you and what do you want?' she demanded. The man motioned her to pick up a candle and follow him. He

OPPOSITE: The imposing red
sandstone Powis Castle, with its
wonderful gardens and parkland,
is worth visiting, and its helpful
ghost seems to be at rest.

RIGHT: Tangled undergrowth
threatens to overwhelm the
remains of Ewloe Castle, and
there are times when strange
lights dance over its walls.

led her to a small room and, stooping down, lifted one of the floorboards to reveal a locked casket underneath. He then showed her a crevice in the wall where its key was concealed.

'Both casket and key must be taken out and sent to the earl in London,' he informed her. 'Do this and I will trouble the house no more.' With that, he turned and walked from the room.

The old woman (who, considering the prank that the servants had evidently played on her, could be forgiven for wishing them to be as troubled as possible) appears to have been willing to let bygones be bygones. Rousing the servants, she told them what had happened. A quick search soon revealed the hidden key and casket, both of which were despatched to their master in London. Although he never revealed the contents, the earl was so delighted that he provided for the woman from that day forth so that she never again wanted for any creature comfort. The ghost's mission was evidently accomplished, for he has never since returned to the castle which, despite possessing a veritable labyrinth of creepy, dark corridors and tapestry-hung rooms, is more than content to let board-lifting phantoms remain firmly in its past.

EWLOE CASTLE
Ewloe, Nr Hawarden, Clwyd Ⓐ
THE WOOD-BOUND SPECTRE.

The ruins of Ewloe Castle are cloaked in secrecy and exude an air of timeless mystery. The castle began life as a Norman manor house, and was converted into a stone castle in the early 1200s by Llewelyn the Great. The wood-bound ruins now crouch in their sleepy hollow. Long abandoned as a place of human habitation, its occupants now are earthbound wraiths whose nebulous activities have been known to elicit cold shivers even on the brightest summer's day. A glowing spectre swathed in white has been seen strolling about the ramparts. Whatever or whoever it is or, more pertinently, was, it

possesses a menacing aura that strikes terror into stunned witnesses. On one occasion, the fearsome phantom so startled a dog that the petrified pooch never recovered from its shock and died two days later. Witnesses have heard the measured tread of soldiers marching in the woodland that surrounds the castle, and ghostly lights have been reported dancing over the walls and towers. There is also ghostly singing that drifts down from the ramparts. It is so loud that it is clearly audible over the thunderstorms favoured by the phantom crooner as his background accompaniment.

RUTHIN CASTLE
Ruthin, Clwyd 🛏
HAUNTED HOSPITALITY

This handsome pile of red sandstone dates from the mid-19th century and is now a delightful hotel basking amid beautiful and peaceful countryside. Yet just a few short steps past the luxuriant gardens, intrepid ghost hunters find themselves poised on the threshold of an underground labyrinth, where dark, dank corridors meander through sinister dungeons and ice-cold moisture drips from above. This strange and chilling place is all that remains of the original castle, one of Edward I's chain of subjugating fortresses, which in 1282 came into the ownership of Reginald de Grey. The wife of his second-in-command is said to haunt the castle and grounds where, due to her somewhat conservative style of dress, she is known simply as the 'Grey Lady'.

Tradition holds that this woman, whose living name is now forgotten, discovered that her husband was enjoying a

ABOVE: Parts of Ruthin Castle have hardly changed since the 13th century, and today present a chilling labrynth where a grey lady walks.

OPPOSITE: A dragon once terrorized the environs of Denbigh, and its slayer gave the castle and town their name. The Goblin Tower of the castle (below) is haunted.

passionate affair with a local lady, and took it upon herself to despatch her rival with an axe. When her dirty deed was discovered the 'Grey Lady' was executed. Because of the heinousness of her crime, she could not be buried in consecrated ground and was therefore laid to rest outside the old castle walls, where a pile of stones is still said to mark her grave. However, her sombre spirit appears to have a propensity to haunt the battlements and medieval chapel. Fortunately the Grey Lady has chosen to undertake her

nebulous wanderings *sans* axe, and is perceived as a harmless wraith, more inclined to bemuse than terrify, although she does leave a cold chill in her spectral wake.

DENBIGH CASTLE
Denbigh, Denbighshire Ⓐ
THE TOWN OF THE DRAGON AND THE REALM OF THE PLAYFUL CHILD

The dramatic ruin of Denbigh Castle stands upon a lofty hilltop 142.5 metres (467 feet) high. It commands its surroundings today just as it did in 1282, when it was built by Henry de Lacy, Earl of Lincoln, and a legion of legends come marching out of its mist-shrouded past. Long ago a ferocious dragon is said to have lived in the vicinity, and was wont to terrorize the neighbourhood with its fire-breathing antics. It fell to Sion Bodiau (Sir John of the Thumbs) – so-called because he had an extra such digit on each hand – to rid the neighbourhood of this dreadful scourge. Marching boldly into the castle, he did battle with the fearsome beast, supposedly chopping off its head while it was gaping at its attacker's extra thumbs! The locals were so overjoyed that they hoisted their hero aloft and paraded him round the town crying, '*Dim bych*', meaning 'No dragon'. It wasn't long before these words had been corrupted to Denbigh.

The ghosts that wander the old castle, needless to say, find it something of a challenge to match such dramatic beginnings, and are content instead to lead relatively unchallenging ethereal existences. A little way below the castle, hemmed in by dark woodland, stands the Goblin Tower, which de Lacy ordered to be built over a spring that provided water for the garrison. His teenage son could not resist the lure of the scaffolding that surrounded the half-built edifice and, while playing on it, lost his balance and fell to his death. His is thought to be the wispy wraith that has been seen gazing mournfully from its hollow windows. However, the identity of the castle's Grey Lady, whose sombre shade has curdled the blood of many a passer-by, is unknown. She remains an enigma, a forgotten former resident, doomed to linger at the spot where she met with some personal tragedy, was deserted by a feckless lover, or was subjected to any one of the sorrowful indignities that have caused a glittering array of such ghostly ladies to drift across the pages of British folklore and legend.

RHUDDLAN CASTLE
Rhuddlan, Denbighshire Ⓐ
THE KNIGHT FROM HELL AND THE GHOSTLY PRINCESS

Built by Edward I as one of a chain of fortresses intended to suppress Welsh nationalism, Rhuddlan Castle is now no more than a squat ruin scattered over a windy hilltop. It dominates the surrounding countryside, a looming mass of purple-grey stone that stands against the leaden sky, and legends aplenty swirl around its decaying walls.

Long ago Erilda, the beautiful daughter of the King of North Wales, was betrothed to Morvern, Prince of South Wales, a union intended to forge a peace between the two nations. One day, while following the royal hunt, the princess became lost and, with darkness falling, terror gripped her soul. Suddenly a figure rode out from the shadows, and

the most handsome knight she had ever seen appeared before her. He lifted her onto his horse and carried her back to her father's castle at Rhuddlan. The anxious king was overjoyed when the black-clad warrior, with the blood-red plume upon his helmet, rode into the courtyard with his daughter. Sadly, though, this was no chivalrous knight, but a fully-fledged demon from hell, determined to wreck the peace between the two nations. To that end he cast a spell upon the princess and she found herself unable to resist when he suggested that she elope with him. As they made their way towards the nearby river, the bold knight reverted to his true form, and the princess recoiled in horror at the slimy, grey creature to which she was about to plight her troth. Moments later Erilda lay dead, stabbed through the heart by a three-pronged spear that sprang from the claw of her hellish tormentor. Lifting her lifeless form in its scaly arms, the creature flung her into the River Clwyd and, with a devilish cackle of grim satisfaction, leapt in after her. Anyone who is tempted to

dismiss the tale as an idle legend, and ponder why the demon didn't just slay the unfortunate Erilda in the forest, should heed the ghostly screams and demonic laughter that have curdled the blood of many a passer-by in the dead of night. Furthermore, had the demon knight done the dastardly deed beneath the forest canopy, he may well have been denied the pleasure of chasing a spectral Erilda round the ramparts of Rhuddlan Castle night after night until such time as hell freezes over!

ABOVE: Rhuddlan sits astride a windy hilltop, where the ghastly demon of hell who duped a princess, still chases his distraught and beautiful quarry.

OPPOSITE: A video still of Caernarfon Castle that was filmed by an American tourist, featuring the ghost in the doorway (small picture) that looks "like a small king" – one of the many Princes of Wales invested there, perhaps.

CAERNARFON CASTLE
Caernarfon, Gwynedd Ⓐ
THE GHOST POSES

The mighty bulk of Caernarfon Castle rises high over the waters of the Menai Strait, its forbidding walls intended by Edward I to be an imposing symbol of his conquest of Wales. It was here in 1968 that Charles Windsor was invested as Prince of Wales, one of a long line of English royalty to occupy that exalted position. The first Prince of Wales was born in a tiny room in the castle's Eagle Tower, and was the son of Edward I and his wife Eleanor of Castille. Edward had sent Eleanor to Caernarfon in order that their child might be born on Welsh soil. When news was brought to him that his wife had given birth to a son, he was so delighted that he knighted the messenger on the spot. Hurrying to Caernarfon he embraced both his wife and heir and summoned the chieftains of North Wales in order that they might pay homage.

The chieftains implored Edward to appoint a Prince of Wales who might rule over them in his name, and asked that it be someone who could speak neither French nor English, whose character was beyond reproach, whose blood was royal and who had been born in Wales. Edward agreed and presented his newborn son, observing that not only was the baby's character

> ## 'A SMALL KING, WITH HIS SCEPTRE, A CROWN AND A CLOAK ON.'
>
> WITNESS OF A GHOST IN 2001 AT CAERNARFON CASTLE

irreproachable, but he had been born on Welsh soil, was of royal blood and certainly could not speak either French or English. Accepting that they had been tricked, but both unwilling and unable to argue, the Welsh chieftains knelt and kissed the infant's hands.

On the 11th August 2001, an American tourist, Kristi Ormand from Dallas, Texas, visited Caernarfon Castle and climbed to the top of the Eagle Tower, from where she proceeded to take photographs of the castle interior. Although she saw nothing at the time, she was aware of 'feeling a presence' but believed it to be caused by the history that surrounded her. When she returned to America and began downloading her images, she noticed that one photograph showed a strange white figure surrounded by a blue mist, standing in a castle doorway. On closer inspection she thought it looked like, 'a small king, with his sceptre, a crown and a cloak on'. None of her other photographs showed the image, although it did appear on a videotape she had taken of the same doorway. The photograph has since been the subject of animated debate among ghost enthusiasts. Some believe that Kristi may well have caught a spectral apparition on camera, while others attribute it to either lens flare or some reflective, though non-ghostly, object that was in the vicinity of the doorway at the time.

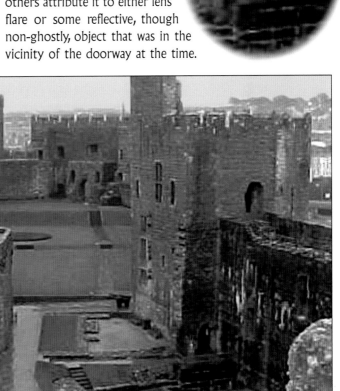

BANSHEES, BOGARTS *and* BRIDES *of* *the* NIGHT

They took her lightly back
Between the night and morrow,
They thought that she was fast asleep,
But she was dead with sorrow.
They have kept her ever since
Deep within the lake,
On a bed of flag-leaves,
Watching till she wake.

FROM THE FAIRIES
by WILLIAM ALLINGHAM (1824–89)

IRELAND

There are more castles in Ireland than in the whole of Wales, England, and Scotland. Between the late 1100s and the early 1700s, over 3,000 castles were constructed there. Yet the majority were not built by the Irish themselves. As a result, the sad remnants and derelict piles that litter the landscape, both in the north and south of the country, are often regarded as symbols of subjugation, which is exactly what they were intended to be. Most stand derelict in the middle of fields, others balance precariously on the edges of cliffs, or are squeezed between (or even incorporated into) later buildings. Quite a lot were burnt down in the early 1920s, during the Irish struggle for independence. Some have undergone tasteful restoration in recent years, while others have been embellished, modernized and altered beyond recognition.

The Irish gift for storytelling has imbued many of the foreign-built castles with a rich array of phantoms, and it is a truly wonderful experience to be regaled with the tales of the ghosts that wander the castles of Ireland.

KEY

1. Castle Donovan
2. Ballinacarriga Castle
3. Thoor Ballylee
4. Leap Castle
5. Kinnitty Castle
6. Charleville Castle
7. Foulksrath Castle
8. Huntingdon Castle
9. Malahide Castle
10. Castle Leslie
11. Carrickfergus Castle
12. Dunluce Castle

CASTLE DONOVAN
Drimoleague, County Cork ®
THE PATHETIC DRIP

Nothing save a hollow, crumbling shell now survives of what was once the principle seat of the O'Donovan clan. The castle was built in 1560 and stands upon a very solid rocky foundation. There is a constant drip of water from the ceiling of the ground-floor chamber. Come winter or summer, rain or shine, the steady trickle continues unabated and has done so for as long as anybody can remember. It is known as the *braon sinnsear*, and tradition says that it is caused by an event that took place in the long-vanished rooms above. The then lord of Castle Donovan is reputed to have owed money to a lady named Dorothy Forde. With her family pressing for repayment, his lordship invited her to his castle to discuss the debt. No sooner had she set foot in the upper chamber than she was seized by assembled members of the O'Donovan clan, and hanged from one of the beams. Ever since, so the legend goes, her teardrops have fallen as the constant drip, a poignant reminder of that brutal act by which her family were deprived of their rightful dues.

BALLINACARRIGA CASTLE
Nr Dunmanway, County Cork
FOUL-SMELLING PHOOKA

The Irish name of this four-storey tower is *Beal na Carraige*, meaning 'the mouth or passage of rock'. It is perched upon a rocky prominence overlooking Ballinacarriga Lough, and can be visited by obtaining the key from the nearby village pub! An unusual feature of its crumbling interior is the number of important stone carvings, mostly of a religious nature, that can be seen around the walls of what was the third floor. On one window arch is a depiction of Christ on the cross between two thieves, and nearby are carved a crown of thorns, a hammer and a heart pierced with two swords. Another window contains the initials R.M.C.C., together with the date 1585. These are believed to be the initials of Randal Murlihy and his wife Catharine Cullinane and the date when the building was erected. Opposite is the carved figure of a woman with five roses, which local tradition claims represents Catharine Cullinane and her five children, but which is more likely to depict the Blessed Virgin.

The roof and parapets of the castle were long ago removed by a garrison of Cromwellian troops who had occupied the fortress for a time and who, as was their custom, took down the overhanging parapets in order to render the building defenceless. Enough of the fortification remains to provide the visitor with a good impression of what it was like to live in a medieval castle. It was an age when belief in a darker side of

ABOVE: A single wall of what was once the seat of a proud clan is all that remains of Castle Donovan, where a shameful murder took place long ago.

BELOW: The four-storey keep of Ballinacarriga Castle is where to meet a phooka, the most dreaded Irish spectre.

PREVIOUS PAGES: Shattered Dunluce Castle enjoys a dramatic situation and unthreatening 'presences'.

ABOVE: The stern tower of Thoor Ballylee, in its tranquil setting, was once owned by the Irish poet, W.B. Yeats, and some believe it is haunted by his son.

BELOW: W.B. Yeats, had a taste for the occult and was certain that Thoor Ballylee was haunted by a soldier.

OPPOSITE: Leap Castle is acknowledged to be Ireland's most haunted castle; some ghosts are resident, others visit.

nature had a firm grip on the human imagination and it was well known that harmful spirits roamed the night, intent on inflicting injury on any humans that chanced to cross their evil path.

Built into the thickness of the second-floor wall there is a mural gallery, which leads the intrepid visitor to the garderobe, or lavatory, which stands over a chute known as 'Moll the phooka's hole'. Phookas were the most feared of all the creatures that prowled the night. They were strange and evil beings, with male heads and the bodies of a goat, horse or dog. They could fly short distances, although they had no wings, were extremely ugly and ill-tempered and generally to be avoided at all costs. They ran in packs, and their sole desire was to inflict harm — upon defenceless humans, causing crops to fail, children to die suddenly or, worst of all, to steal newborn babies. Irish peasants would ascribe accidental falls to the malign influence of a phooka. Ruined or wrecked castles were associated with them, the foul-smelling chute of a garderobe being the ideal portal by which these dreaded creatures could gain access and wreak their devilish mayhem upon the inhabitants.

THOOR BALLYLEE
Nr Gort, County Galway Ⓐ
YEATS'S HAUNTED HOME

I declare this tower is my symbol; I declare
This winding, gyring spiring treadmill of a stair is my
Ancestral stair.
From *Blood and the Moon* **by W. B. Yeats**

Once known as Islandmore Castle, this evocative and atmospheric stone tower with its narrow and time-worn stairs was a virtual ruin when the poet W.B. Yeats (1865–1939) purchased it in 1917 for the nominal sum of £35. Yeats renamed the building *Thoor* (being the Irish for tower) Ballylee, commenting that, ' I think the harsh sound of Thoor amends the softness of the rest'. Following considerable restoration, the property was finally habitable in 1919 when it became his summer residence and, thereafter, a central symbol of his poetry. Yeats was a devotee of the occult, once observing that, 'The mystical life is the centre of all that I do and all that I think and all that I write'. He believed implicitly in the existence of ghosts and was convinced that the tower was haunted by an Anglo-Norman soldier. A later curator was also convinced that a spectral form wandered the worn stairway of the tower, and was reluctant to ascend it as the day turned into night. Her suspicions were evidently shared by her pet dog who would frequently appear terrified of something it could apparently see in the downstairs rooms.

One summer's afternoon in 1989, an English family touring County Galway arrived at the tower as it was closing. As they wished to photograph Yeats's sitting room, the curator obligingly reopened the window shutters so that a picture could be taken. The husband, David Blinkthorne, stayed alone in the room to take several photographs while his family went off to explore the rest of the building. When the film was

developed, Mr Blinkthorne was astonished to see on one of the prints the ghostly silhouette of what appeared to be a young boy, standing in front of the camera. No one else had been in the room when the photograph was taken, and none of the other prints showed the strange and inexplicable apparition. The ghostly boy's identity still remains a mystery, although some have suggested that it may have been Yeats's own son.

LEAP CASTLE
Nr Birr, County Offaly Ⓐ Ⓣ
THE MOST HAUNTED CASTLE IN IRELAND

In May 2002, Sean Ryan, a world-class musician, and owner of Leap Castle along with his wife Anne, found a ghostly old man sitting in a chair by a downstairs fireplace. Having bade his phantom guest, 'Good day', Sean continued about his business. After all, a new ghost dropping by unannounced is just part of life's rich tapestry when you happen to live in what has long been considered Ireland's most haunted castle.

Standing upon a vast throne of solid rock, Leap Castle was once the stronghold of the warlike O'Carrolls, and its eventful history is mostly written in their blood. In the 16th century, O'Carroll of the Leap held a lavish banquet at his family fortress and invited a rural branch of his own sept (Irish clan) to partake of his hospitality. No sooner had the unfortunate guests sat down to dinner than he massacred every one of them. Inter-clan bloodshed was a common occurrence and members of the tribe attended family get-togethers or reunions at their peril! Following the death of Mulrooney O'Carroll in 1532, a bitter dispute over succession arose. As siblings battled each other for leadership of the clan, 'one-eyed' Teige O'Carroll is said to have slain his own brother, who was also a priest, as he celebrated mass in the 'bloody chapel'.

However, the days of O'Carroll occupancy were drawing to a close, and they were about to lose possession in a suitably bloodthirsty manner. A 17th-century daughter of the clan fell in love with an English soldier named Captain Darby, who was being held prisoner in the castle dungeons. She smuggled food to him and eventually engineered his escape. As they were making their way down the staircase, her brother suddenly confronted them, and the captain silenced him with a single sword thrust. As his lover then became the heiress to Leap Castle, it passed into the ownership of the captain's family when the two were married.

The last of his descendants to own Leap Castle was Jonathan Charles Darby who arrived on 16th July 1880. In 1909, his wife Mildred wrote an article for the *Occult Review* describing how she had held several séances at the castle during which she had attracted the unwelcome attentions of an elemental – a primitive and malevolent force that attaches itself to a particular place. Mildred Darby described how she was 'standing in the gallery looking down at the main floor, when I felt somebody put a hand on my shoulder. The thing was the size of a sheep. Thin, gaunt and shadowy... its eyes, which seemed half-

decomposed in black cavities, stared into mine. The horrible smell... gave me a deadly nausea. It was the smell of a decomposing corpse...' Mildred's occult dabbling also appears to have awoken other malevolent forces within the walls of Leap Castle, and it was at this time that its fearsome reputation became firmly established.

Following the castle's destruction by fire in 1922, workmen who had commenced gutting the interior discovered an *oubliette* – a small dungeon whose name, derived from the French *oublier,* meaning 'forget', says it all – behind a wall of the bloody chapel. This sinister little room was crammed with the mortal remains of the unfortunate victims of Leap Castle's bloody and brutal past, and three cartloads of human bones were eventually cleared away from this ghastly charnel house.

Over the next 70 years, Leap remained an empty shell, its fearsome reputation ensuring that the locals shunned it, particularly at night when all manner of ghostly activity was known to stir within its moss-clad walls. From across the fields people would watch the window of the 'bloody chapel' suddenly light up, as though hundreds of flickering candles were blazing within. Some, who dared walk among the ruins, experienced alarming encounters with a lustrous lady wearing a billowing red gown.

In 1972, the castle was purchased by an Australian of Irish descent who sold it to Sean and Anne Ryan in 1991, and Sean set about converting the ruin into a habitable family home. Shortly afterwards, restoration was suddenly halted when the ladder he was working from was inexplicably pushed away, from the wall, forcing him to jump down several storeys and sustain a fractured knee. No sooner had he resumed work than another freak accident caused him to break an ankle. 'We began to think that we weren't welcome here,' Anne Ryan stoically observed.

Today, though, the spirits have come to accept the present-day inhabitants of the castle and appear content to exist alongside Sean and Anne. They may make nuisances of themselves occasionally, but on the whole they are no longer malevolent. The sound of traditional music now wafts beneath the rafters as Sean entertains guests and visitors both on tours and at storytelling nights. And should a stray sprite or forlorn phantom choose to make an appearance, they are more than welcome to pull up a chair and enjoy the atmosphere of the place that they have helped imbue with the reputation of being Ireland's most haunted castle.

KINNITTY CASTLE
Kinnitty, County Offaly
HAUNT OF THE MONASTIC SOOTHSAYER

Nestling amid the foothills of the Slieve Bloom mountains, the Gothic revival Kinnitty Castle has had a long and turbulent history. The first stronghold built on the site was destroyed in 1209 and rebuilt by the Normans in 1213. In time, it came into the possession of the powerful O'Carrolls of Ely. In 1630, one of their line, William O'Carroll, built a new fortress, which was confiscated by the English. In 1664, the estate was granted to Colonel Thomas Winter as a reward for his military service and almost 200 years later, his descendants sold it to the Bernard family. In 1811, Lady Catherine Hutchinson, wife of Thomas Bernard, commissioned the present castle. Although the building was burnt by the Republicans in 1922, it was restored and has since been transformed into the magnificent, extremely cosy, hotel whose dark, atmospheric corridors, elegant rooms, library bar resplendent with rows of antique books, and sweeping stairways, provide visitors with a tranquil haven from the cares of the modern world.

Still in existence in the extensive grounds are the remains an Augustinian abbey and an ancient Celtic high cross, carved with depictions of Adam and Eve and intertwined birds, together with Christ's presentation in the temple and the crucifixion. It would also appear that one of the long-dead monks from the old foundation finds the ambience of the castle more than congenial, and chooses to wander the darker recesses of the banqueting room. From here he delights in revealing future events linked with the everyday business of the hotel, to one particular member of staff who often astonishes the owner with the accuracy of the prophecies!

CHARLEVILLE FOREST CASTLE
Nr Tullamore, County Offaly Ⓐ Ⓣ

IRELAND'S SCARIEST CASTLE?

A sense of genuine antiquity prevails over the sylvan landscape that cradles Ireland's most enigmatic and impressive Gothic revival castle. Charleville is approached via a long and pitted drive that meanders through sinister tunnels of massive oaks whose crooked shadows dance before you, their writhing forms beckoning you onwards. As your nebulous escorts fall suddenly away you are confronted by an awesome vision of breathtaking splendour, as unyielding walls, punctured by mullioned windows and crowned by towering turrets, loom gracefully over you.

Charleville Forest Castle was built between 1798 and 1812 by Charles William Bury (1764–1835), the first Earl of Charleville, and designed by Francis Johnston. It is a proud testimony to the designer's vision, and the sheer extravagance — unhindered by the constraints of their purse strings — with which successive generations of the Charleville family have enthusiastically embraced life. Every so often, the pressure of living beyond their means would necessitate the temporary closure of the castle. Subsequent reopenings, though, would often be marked by a suitably flamboyant gesture, such as engaging the talents of Arts and Crafts Movement supremo William Morris, much of whose exquisite dining-room ceiling work amazingly still survives. The family's inability to curb their excesses eventually resulted in periods of occupancy becoming more intermittent until, by the early 1960s, Charleville had been all but abandoned.

It is now owned by Bridget Vance, a charismatic American who is slowly rousing the castle from its slumber. With the aid of local craftsmen, she is restoring its echoing rooms to their past grandeur. As her family go about their task, the spirits of bygone residents have begun to stir, and an abundance of

ABOVE: Those who climb the Grand Staircase at Charleville Forest Castle may feel an unnerving and chilly rush of air as a ghostly presence brushes by them.

OPPOSITE: Gothic in both style and atmosphere, Kinnitty Castle is graced with the ghost of a prophetic monk.

ghosts now wander through what has recently been dubbed 'Ireland's spookiest castle'. The silence of the early hours is sometimes shattered by the playful whoops of children, enjoying a phantom game in what was once the nursery. It

heads suddenly switched on, and at the same moment a radio in the room next door — which was definitely empty at the time — began blaring out classical music.

The wraiths of both Charles William Bury and Francis Johnston have also been seen here. One morning, at around 3am, Bridget Vance's late mother, Connie, awoke to find them leading a ghostly cavalcade across her bedroom in the tower. It consisted of a woman in a black hood, a little girl and a group of around 17 'monks or druids' who encircled her bed and appeared to bestow a blessing upon her.

The most poignant of all the spectres that walk this most haunting and atmospheric of castles is that of the little girl in a blue chiffon dress. Her shimmering shade has been seen many times on the great, winding staircase, the faded walls and creaking boards of which are imbued with a decidedly chilling aura. Her name in life was Harriet, and one day she was sent upstairs to wash her hands. Having done so, she was playfully sliding down the balustrade when she lost her balance and plunged to her death on the floor below. Many people walking down the staircase where the tragedy occurred have felt the cold draught of her invisible presence as she brushes past them, while others have seen her phantom form skipping playfully in front of them. The ghost of a small boy occasionally joins her. Once, when Bridget's son was around three years old, he went missing. Fearful of the steep stairs and precarious drops around the property, the family began an anxious search. They eventually found him at the bottom of the stairwell where he told how 'the little boy and girl' had looked after him as he came down the stairs.

Charleville Forest Castle is a welcoming place. The abundance of ghosts that roam its corridors are, on the whole, friendly, and you leave the castle with a sense of sheer wonder. But as you make your way back along the driveway, you come upon an ancient reminder of the castle's more sinister past. Towering over you, its lower branches almost touching the road, is the prodigious 'king oak', the massive girth of which testifies to its venerable age. Yet its majestic splendour is tinged with a fearsome reputation, for it was always maintained that whenever one of its branches fell, a member of the Charleville family would die. In May 1963, a huge bolt of lightning smashed into it and shattered its trunk from top to bottom. Although the oak survived, relief was muted when, two weeks later, Colonel Charles Howard-Bury, the head of the family and the last of the line to own the castle, suddenly dropped dead.

FOULKSRATH CASTLE
Nr Kilkenny, County Kilkenny
THE GHOST ON THE STAIRS

Named after Fulco De La Frene, the 13th-century founder of the settlement, and builder of the first castle on the site, Foulksrath Castle basks in peaceful seclusion amid serenely beautiful

ABOVE: The solid stone tower of Foulksrath Castle now houses a youth hostel...and a pair of ghosts who were the result of a brutal act and a teenage tantrum.

OPPOSITE: In the 17th-century Huntingdon Castle (bottom), hangs a portrait of a woman (top) who married into the family and whose ghost still roams the corridors.

may be these same children who were once responsible for locking Bridget's daughter, Kate, in a dark cupboard in their playroom. Older revenants appear to have been to blame for disturbing Richard Hayes who, following a party at the castle, placed his bedroll on the floor and settled down to sleep. Next morning, the children asked why he had slept with the door open and the lights on? He revealed that just as he was nodding off, two elderly English men — who, from the style of their speech, were evidently of another era — had struck up an animated conversation, interspersed with the downing of copious amounts of alcohol. Although he could hear them close by, he could not see them!

I too experienced an inexplicable incident when I visited the castle. I was talking with Kate, who asked me if I had ever seen a ghost. As I began to answer, the huge chandelier above our countryside. It is a solid stone building of atmospheric rooms that now functions as a delightful hostel operated by the Irish Youth Organization, *An Oige*. Although Fulco De La Frene was killed in a neighbourhood skirmish in 1349, and his castle replaced with the present fortress in the 16th century, his actions have, apparently, left behind a psychic imprint that has imbued the shadowy recesses of one of the upper rooms with a spectre of regular habits. On 29th November each year, the silence of the early morning is broken by the sound of footsteps echoing from the darkness. A door is heard to open and then close as an invisible revenant makes its annual return to the place where its living self met with a violent death at the hands of the castle's founder. Tradition holds that this mysterious visitor is the ghost of a sentry who fell asleep one night while on guard duty. Unfortunately for him, Fulco De La Frene, a man not known for his pacifist pursuits, chose to undertake a tour of inspection at that moment. Stumbling upon the slumbering form, he was furious at such a blatant dereliction of duty. Grabbing hold of the sleeping soldier, he pitched the poor man to his death from the top of the building. Henceforth, the soldier's ghost has made an annual pilgrimage to the site of his ignoble end.

Elsewhere, the winding stairway that delivers the visitor to the upper reaches of the building is the haunt of a ghostly, though invisible, lady. She is said to have been a daughter of the castle who once fell in love with a lowly soldier and was forbidden to see him again by her irate father. In a tantrum, she raced screaming down the stairs, but tripped over her skirts, and tumbling headlong to the bottom, broke her neck. But her unseen ghost is still said to wander up and down the old stairs where she announces her presence with the sweet fragrance of wild flowers, a sudden drop in temperature and the gentle flapping of her skirts upon the stones as she prepares to undergo her fatal fall, time and time again.

HUNTINGDON CASTLE
Clonegal, County Carlow Ⓐ Ⓣ
THE PHANTOM BISHOP, AND THE WAITING WIFE

Huntingdon Castle as it stands today is a Jacobean gesture in architecture. It was built in 1625 by the 1st Lord Esmonde, and replaced an earlier stronghold that had been built in the 15th century on the site of an ancient monastery. Approached via a long avenue of majestic limes, it casts a long finger of shadow across its surroundings, and possesses a spellbinding quality. Its interior of dark, creaking corridors and atmospheric rooms, crammed with an eclectic mix of tapestries, suits of armour, dusty old books, stuffed animals and family portraits, has a decided otherworldly feel. It comes as little surprise, therefore, to learn that this truly mysterious castle, which for over 200 years has been home to the Durdin-Robertson family, is haunted. Outside is the 600-year-

old yew walk, one of the few survivors from the days of the monastery. Its entwined branches form a long and mysterious tunnel that could so easily be a gateway into another time. On several occasions, monks manage to transcend the centuries, and their ghostly forms are seen walking up and down beneath the interlocking canopy. Elsewhere in the gardens, the restless wraith of Ailish O'Flaherty, the first wife of Lord Esmonde, is sometimes seen standing by the 'spy bush', combing her long hair by moonlight and wailing in grief-stricken anguish. Her husband and son went off to the wars, and here she would stand, anxiously awaiting their return.

A spectral soldier has been known to knock on the castle door. He is thought to have lived in the 17th century, when Cromwell's forces were riding roughshod over the land. Having disguised himself in the uniform of the Royalist opposition, the soldier set off to gather information about the enemy. On his return, his comrades failed recognize him and shot him dead through the grille of the door, where his ghostly face is now sometimes seen.

Crossing the threshold, a portrait of Barbara St Lege (1748–1820) hangs on one of the walls inside. She married into the family and was, apparently, so taken with Huntingdon

Castle that her spirit still walks the corridors, jangling her keys. She is closely followed by her maidservant, Honor Byrne, who pauses to polish door handles with her hair. Bishop Leslie of Limerick, who stayed at the castle when he retired in the 18th century, haunts the 'four-poster room'. Several guests have woken in the dead of night to find his genial phantom standing at the foot of the bed. A portrait of a Spanish flower girl gazes from the wall of the room and, from time to time, the bishop's face has been known to replace hers.

Huntingdon Castle is a magical and timeless place that possesses a unique atmosphere. It is a tranquil time capsule that is truly one of Ireland's most historical and fascinating treasures.

MALAHIDE CASTLE
Malahide, County Dublin Ⓐ
PUCK THE PHANTOM SENTRY

Malahide is a stunningly picturesque fortress that stands amid a profusion of massive oaks, mighty chestnuts and towering sycamores 14.5 kilometres (9 miles) to the north of Dublin. Richard Talbot, who had been awarded the Lordship of

ABOVE: Malahide is a big castle with a little ghost – of a man who even has his own miniature doorway through which to make his spectral entrance.

Malahide by Henry II, built the first castle on the site in about 1185. Thereafter, despite regular sieges and constant warring aimed at displacing them, his descendants clung to possession for 791 years (apart from a ten-year eviction during the Cromwellian era). In 1975, the Hon. Rose Talbot was forced to sell her ancestral home to pay the exorbitant death duties occasioned by the sudden demise of her brother Milo, the last Lord Talbot de Malahide, in 1973. Purchased by the local authority, the castle was opened to the public. Visitors can now experience its majestic ambience, and wander along the ancient corridors and winding stairways that lead to atmospheric old rooms, resplendent with period furnishings, family portraits and intriguing artefacts.

Having ascended the stone stairway from the reception area, you step into the Oak Room, which sits at the heart of the medieval castle. Above the fireplace is a 16th-century Flemish carving depicting the Coronation of the Virgin. One of the castle's most abiding legends centres upon this exquisite work. In August 1649, Oliver Cromwell invaded Ireland with a force of some 12,000 soldiers. The then owner of Malahide, John Talbot, was evicted and Cromwell gave the fortress to loyal supporter, Miles Corbet. Tradition asserts that the moment that Corbet took possession, the carving mysteriously disappeared and was not seen for ten years, until, following the restoration of Charles II in 1660 and the subsequent execution of Corbet, the castle was restored to the Talbots, whereupon the carving reappeared upon the wall!

The Great Hall of the castle is one of the most important medieval rooms in Ireland and has remained virtually unaltered since its construction in 1475. On 30th June 1690, 14 members of the family took breakfast here before setting off the following day, to fight in the Battle of the Boyne, at which every one of them was killed.

To the right of the minstrels' gallery in the hall, there is a tiny doorway around which the castle's most famous and irrepressible spectral inhabitant has been known to manifest itself. Known as Puck to generations of residents, he stands just 1.2 metres (4 feet) tall and is blessed with a long, straggly beard. No-one knows for certain who he was, but there is a tradition that he lived in the 15th century. Because of his slight stature, he was deemed unsuitable as a fighting man so was employed instead as a watchman. Unfortunately, he was partial to the odd tipple and one night, having imbibed a little too liberally, fell asleep at his post and failed to spot that an enemy was about to storm the castle. Shamed by his neglect of duty, the remorseful sentry hanged himself from the minstrels' gallery. His spirit has remained here ever since and appears whenever there are changes of which he disapproves. The last sighting was in 1976, when the castle's fixtures and fittings were to be sold. A London auctioneer was compiling an inventory when he looked up from his work and saw the unmistakable figure of Puck, standing by the tiny doorway, shaking his head in censure.

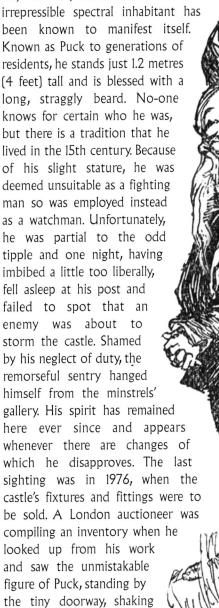

CASTLE LESLIE
Glaslough, County Monaghan 🛏
THE HAUNTED RED ROOM

When Paul McCartney and Heather Mills chose Castle Leslie as the venue for their wedding on 11th June 2002, they were following an illustrious cast of bygone guests that have included Dean Swift, W.B. Yeats, Sir John Betjeman and fellow rocker Mick Jagger.

It was Sir John Leslie who was responsible for rebuilding the old castle in 1878, largely at the insistence of his pretty young wife Constance. As Sir John grew older, his wife came to detest the sight of him and designed a huge floral arrangment that could hide him from her view at the dinner table. The couple moved to London in 1910 and, following her death there in 1925, Lady Constance's ghost was seen walking round the castle by the servants and has been seen several times since.

It is the Red Room, however, whose four-poster bed has been described as a 'doorway in and out of this life... born in and died in', that is the castle's most haunted room. It was here that Lady Marjorie Leslie saw the ghost of her son, Norman, who had been killed in action during World War I. Shortly afterwards Lady Marjorie awoke one night to find Norman's ghost standing by the chest of drawers, surrounded by a 'cloud of light', leafing

'WHY NORMAN – WHAT ARE YOU DOING HERE?'

LADY MARJORIE TO THE GHOST OF HER SON IN CASTLE LESLIE'S RED ROOM

ABOVE: Paul and Heather McCartney were married at Castle Leslie, but whether they saw the ghost of World War I soldier Norman Leslie, is not known.

OPPOSITE: Carrickfergus Castle goes back to the 1100s, but the ghost that returns to it is that of an 18th-century soldier, who was the victim of mistaken identity.

through some letters, apparently seeking one in particular. Sitting up she asked him, 'Why Norman – what are you doing here?' He turned, smiled and faded slowly away. Since then, several guests spending the night in that room have seen his ghost rummaging through the chest of drawers.

CARRICKFERGUS CASTLE
Carrickfergus, County Antrim Ⓐ
BUTTONCAPS WELL

The imposing fortress of Carrickfergus Castle sits atop a jagged knoll. The building's origins stretch back to 1185, when Anglo-Norman adventurers rode roughshod over the country, carving out large chunks of land on which to establish family estates and dynastic fortunes. One such buccaneer was John de Courcy, a Norman lord who had heard a prophecy that Ulster would one day be conquered by a white knight from a foreign land, riding a white horse, with birds of prey upon his shield. Since he was fair-haired, de Courcy became convinced that he was the knight of whom the legend spoke. Thus, mounted upon a white warhorse and

bearing a shield emblazoned with heraldic birds, he led a small band of well-armed soldiers into Ulster and began a campaign of bloody conquest that lasted for over a quarter of a century. Each victory was consolidated with the building of a castle, such as the one at Carrickfergus, which now has the distinction of being the oldest intact stone castle in Ireland. In 1210, the castle was taken over by King John who made it an administrative centre for English government, in which capacity it served for the next seven centuries.

There is a deep, dark well in the castle, around which the ghostly apparition of a soldier is said to appear. A tragic tale of love and betrayal, culminating in a monumental miscarriage of justice, is said to lie behind the haunting.

Robert Rainey, a soldier stationed at Carrickfergus Castle around the 1760s, was a man with a wild reputation. But when he met and fell in love with a local girl named Betsy Baird, he vowed to forsake his wayward ways if she would marry him. He was overjoyed when she consented. Unbeknown to Rainey, Betsy was also involved with the brother of his commanding officer, a Colonel Jennings. How Rainey discovered his fiancée's infidelity is unknown, but when he did, his reaction was one of uncontrollable fury. He encountered his rival on the road outside and ran him through with his sword. Calmly sheathing his weapon, he returned to his quarters, washed away the incriminating bloodstains, and retired to bed. Jennings, however, lived long enough to tell his brother what had happened. The only problem was that he named his assailant as a certain Timothy Lavery, who was also stationed at the castle, and who bore an uncanny resemblance to the true attacker, Rainey. The unfortunate Lavery was charged with murder and, despite protestations of innocence, was found guilty and sentenced to death. As the noose was placed around his neck he summoned up every last ounce of energy and vowed to haunt the castle. Although Rainey confessed the truth many years later, Timothy Lavery's indignant spectre was unimpressed and continues to hover around the old well, which some call 'Buttoncaps Well' in his honour. This was his nickname in life, because of the large button he wore at the centre of his cap.

DUNLUCE CASTLE
Nr Portrush, County Antrim Ⓐ
A SPRAWLING MASS OF HAUNTED STONE

Protected by sheer cliffs and sprawled across a sea-sprayed dias, the gaunt shell of Dunluce Castle is a reminder of wilder, more violent times, and few castles can boast an aspect that is more awesome or dramatic. Its soaring ramparts and shattered turrets, punctured by the eyeless slits of hollow windows, look down upon pebbled pathways that snake their way into roofless rooms, whose lichen-covered walls hold thousands of memories. The first castle to be erected on the site was built

ABOVE: The fabric of Dunluce Castle is shattered by time, but, in its spectacular cliff-top position, it still evokes its turbulent past – and shelters a pony-tailed phantom.

by the MacQuillans in the 14th century, and it is possible that the outer walls with the two round towers date from their tenure. The ghostly White Lady, whose nebulous shade wanders the north-east tower, is believed to have been a daughter of the family. Her father forbade her from marrying the man she loved, causing her to pine away there and die of a broken heart.

In the 16th century, the castle came into the possession of the MacDonnells, and it is with their occupancy that its history is most indelibly linked. Sorley Boy MacDonnell (1505–89) inherited the family's Irish estates in 1556. He was taken prisoner by his brother-in-law, Shane O'Neill, at the battle of Glentaisie in 1565. He was held captive for two years before his kinsmen set him free, having murdered Shane during a banquet called to negotiate a truce between the two families.

In 1584, Queen Elizabeth I's Lord Deputy of Ireland, Sir John Perrot, brought an army to Dunluce and battered the garrison

into submission with a relentless bombardment of cannon fire. Having evicted Sorley Boy, he installed Peter Carey as constable of the castle. Queen Elizabeth, however, was furious at the unnecessary expedition and, in 1586, granted the castle back to Sorley Boy who celebrated his arrival by hanging the unfortunate Carey from the ramparts of the south-east tower. Spurred on, no doubt, by the indignity of his demise, Carey's ghostly figure, clad in a purple cloak and sporting a ponytail, has wandered the tower ever since.

In 1635, Sorley Boy's grandson, Randall, married Catherine Manners, the widow of the Duke of Buckingham, and brought her to live at Dunluce. This elegant lady was used to the cosseted life of London society, and found her new home something of an ordeal. She hated the place and the constant boom of the sea drove her to distraction. One stormy night in 1639, as the family sat down to dinner, her worst fears were realized when the north wall of the kitchen court collapsed into the sea, taking several servants to a watery grave. She point blank refused to live on the rock again and persuaded her husband to build a new house on the mainland. Although the castle remained habitable for the remainder of the 17th

century, the fact that it ceased to be the main residence of the MacDonnells effectively sounded its death knell. The relentless assault of the elements gradually reduced it to the ruin that it is today, but no visitor can fail to be impressed by its mysterious ambience and dramatic location.

Even though the castle has now settled into a docile old age, past residents still make forays from beyond the grave to remind us of its stormy and eventful past. Several people have reported feeling a cold chill on entering the south-east tower, as if some unseen presence had pushed past them. Staff arriving at the castle's shop in the morning sometimes find that books have been lifted from the shelves and placed neatly on the floor overnight, or radios that were definitely turned off the previous day have been mysteriously switched back on.

Whoever the spirits that now walk the ethereal plain of Dunluce Castle may have been in life, their activities are seldom malicious and rarely inspire fear. Indeed, those who encounter them are more than happy to let them continue about their ghostly business for as long as these ancient walls shall stand.

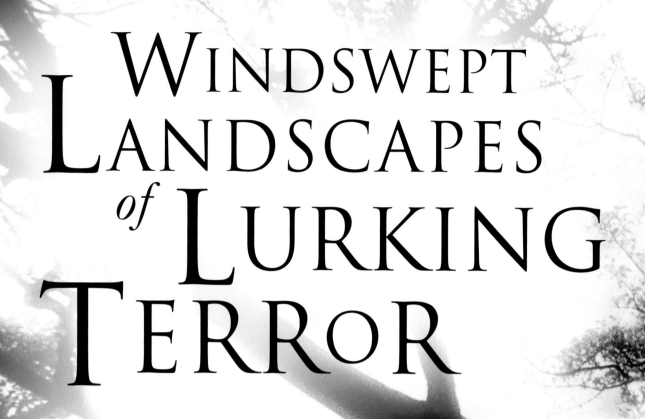

Windswept Landscapes of Lurking Terror

The boast of heraldry, the pomp of pow'r,
And all that beauty, all that wealth e'er gave,
Awaits alike th' inevitable hour.
The paths of glory lead but to the grave.

FROM *ELEGY WRITTEN IN A COUNTRY CHURCHYARD*
BY THOMAS GRAY (1716–71)

NORTH YORKSHIRE, COUNTY DURHAM, CUMBRIA & NORTHUMBERLAND

Travel west through the urban spread and industry of Lancashire and move into the Lake District, and you feel the stresses and strains of the modern world fall away. Suddenly, you find yourself confronted by the awesome grandeur of nature. It is the same in the east of the region where, having journeyed through the tranquil enchantment of Yorkshire, you reach the untamed splendour of Northumbria.

In the past, you would have found in both regions, a wild frontier land that was the lawless domain of savage cattlestealers and ruthless warlords. Consequently, castles were built here long after the need for them had diminished throughout the rest of England and Wales. The memories of these unsettled times linger on in the gaunt ruins and sturdy towers that litter the landscape, and in the ghosts that might be encountered among them. For this is a region that inspires the imagination and, as such, it is a must for all those who seek the more mysterious places of haunted England.

KEY

1. Spofforth Castle
2. Pickering Castle
3. Scarborough Castle
4. Bowes Castle
5. Lumley Castle Hotel
6. Sizergh Castle
7. Carlisle Castle
8. Muncaster Castle
9. Thirlwall Castle
10. Warkworth Castle
11. Chillingham Castle
12. Bamburgh Castle

SPOFFORTH CASTLE
Spofforth, North Yorkshire
A SPECTRAL TUMBLE INTO THE GREAT BEYOND

Dating mostly from the 15th century, the weathered remnants of Spofforth Castle possess an unpretentious ambience that no amount of urban encroachment can subdue. It was once a seat of the powerful Percy family, and the birthplace of Henry Percy who became known as 'Harry Hotspur' (see page 136) because of his courage. Today, however, it is an abandoned relic, cobwebbed with time and haunted by a singularly unusual spectre of decidedly chilling appearance.

It occasionally happens that people approaching the ruins are startled by a female entity of a bluish-white hue that appears momentarily on top of the tower. Suddenly she will throw herself groundwards, the hideous spectacle of the plummeting phantom made even more gruesome by the realization that only the upper half of her body is visible. The lower section chooses to remain in whatever ethereal domain her journey begins. Who she is, or was, or why she felt the need to kill herself, nobody has ever been able to ascertain, because she has the rather annoying habit of disappearing at the moment of impact.

ABOVE: The forbidding outlines of Spofforth Castle in North Yorkshire are gruesomely utilized by half a ghost, a former suicide.

PREVIOUS PAGES: Children tend to fall strangely silent while exploring the shadowy recesses of Warkworth Castle.

PICKERING CASTLE
Pickering, North Yorkshire Ⓐ Ⓔ
THE PHANTOM FOOTSTEPS

The remains of Pickering Castle may not be the most impressive of ruins, but they certainly possess a unique atmosphere. The knowledge that there have been sightings of a robed monk, whose faceless form drifts across the grounds towards the ruined keep, his hands outstretched as though carrying some invisible item, does little to dispel the chilling aura that permeates the very walls of the building. When this book's photographer, John Mason and a female researcher were working at Pickering for the book *Haunted Heritage* in 1999, they were startled by the sound of footsteps moving across the wooden floorboards of the empty first floor of the Diate Hill tower. The custodian was unable to shed any light on the source of the footsteps, but emphatically denied that they could have been caused by any supernatural agent, stating that he didn't believe in ghosts... but adding that he didn't like to hang round the premises after dark!

SCARBOROUGH CASTLE
Scarborough, North Yorkshire Ⓐ Ⓔ
EDWARD II'S PHANTOM FAVOURITE

The magnificent ruin of Scarborough Castle stands on a windswept clifftop, its commanding presence dominating the town and harbour which seem to cower beneath its sullen walls. Begun in the 1130s by Count William of Aumale, it stands on the site of a Roman signal station. Despite sustaining severe damage in the Civil War, it remained in use as a prison and then a barracks, in which capacity it continued until the end of World War I. Today, a mysterious aura radiates around this indefatigable symbol of bygone power, and at least one inhabitant from its chequered past returns here.

Piers Gaveston, the son of a Gascon knight, was the childhood friend and later 'favourite' of the capricious, though ill-fated, King Edward II. An arrogant and boastful man, Gaveston succeeded in turning most of England's nobility into implacable enemies. Their hatred was compounded when Edward appointed Gaveston as his regent when the king crossed the Channel to marry Isabella of France in January 1308. When, at Edward's subsequent coronation, Gaveston was given the honour of carrying the crown of England, the barons were stung into action. Under the leadership of Edward's powerful cousin, Thomas of Lancaster, they demanded that Gaveston should be exiled. Edward refused, and Gaveston's power and influence continued to grow unabated. He delighted in unhorsing aristocratic opponents at tournaments and revelled in heaping insult upon injury by giving them nicknames such as *'le chien noir'* (the Black Dog) for the Earl of Warwick, and the 'Old Hog' for another adversary, Thomas of Lancaster.

Eventually the barons could take no more. In 1312, they revolted against Edward, forcing him to flee to York where he set about raising an army, while Gaveston headed for Scarborough and took refuge behind the walls of the castle. The barons promptly laid siege to Scarborough Castle and, having taken Gaveston prisoner, headed south with their quarry, resting that night at Deddington Castle near Banbury. Next morning Gaveston was told to dress and go down to the courtyard where he was met by a group of armed men. 'You know me,' growled the leader, 'I am the Black Dog.' Mounting Gaveston on a mule they took

ABOVE: Here, at Pickering Castle, this book's photographer John Mason was disturbed by the echo of supernatural footsteps while on location.

BELOW: The skeleton of Scarborough Castle commands the town and harbour, and plays host to headless phantom Piers Gaveston, the one-time favourite of Edward II.

him in mock procession to the Earl of Warwick's castle where Thomas of Lancaster and an assembly of barons sentenced him to death. Gaveston was beheaded in June 1312. It is, however, to Scarborough Castle that his headless spectre chooses to return, and where it attempts to lure unsuspecting visitors over the battlements to an ignoble death.

BOWES CASTLE
Bowes, County Durham Ⓐ Ⓔ
THE LEGIONAIRE GUARDIANS OF ILL-GOTTEN GAINS

Bowes Castle was built in the 12th century on the former site of a Roman fort. It was one of Henry II's great tower keeps and, despite now being in ruins, still has the power to intimidate and command. Tradition holds that towards the end of the Roman occupation of Britain, the garrison here ran amok and indulged in a good deal of looting and pilfering in the locality. The incensed locals retaliated by storming the fort and massacring the garrison, but such was the ingenuity of the Romans that they had already secreted away their ill-gotten gains. The treasure has never been discovered, despite the tantalizing clue afforded by a ghostly gaggle of legionaires that are reputedly seen among the ruins, ritually burying their plunder.

LUMLEY CASTLE
Chester-Le-Street, County Durham ⋈
THE LILY OF LUMLEY

In the 14th century, having obtained consent from Richard II, Sir Ralph Lumley fortified the manor house that had been home to his forebears and created Lumley Castle. Today that same castle is a luxury hotel, catering to the whims of discerning travellers, and home to the tragic ghost of Sir Ralph's first wife who, because of her beauty, is poetically remembered as 'the Lily of Lumley'.

In the reception of Lumley Castle there is a well in which, tradition maintains, a gaggle of ghastly monks ended the life of the celebrated beauty. Lady Lumley had broken away from the orthodox faith and become an adherent to the radical doctrines of John Wycliff (1329–84). One day, when Sir Ralph (who was governor of Berwick-upon-Tweed) was called away on official business, the monks of Durham Cathedral took advantage of his absence to attempt to talk his wife out of her heretical beliefs. When she refused to listen to their pleadings, the brutal brethren decided that murder was the only thing that would save her soul. They therefore lured her to a castle bedroom and hacked her to death. Dragging the

ABOVE: Lumley Castle is a fortified manor house where the 'Lily of Lumley', returns when the waters of the River Wear rise, to bemoan her cruel treatment.

body down the stairs they cast it into the well. Assuming that Sir Ralph might not be forthcoming with gratitude for their chosen method of saving his wife's soul, they took a fatally ill young woman from the village, carried her to a nearby convent, and told the nuns that this was Lady Lumley. When the woman died, the monks were then able to tell Sir Ralph the tragic news of his 'wife's' demise.

Sir Ralph became suspicious and, having made his own enquiries, discovered the awful truth. He sent for the monks and confronted them with his evidence. They pleaded for mercy on the grounds that, by killing his wife, they had saved her soul. Unconvinced, Sir Ralph ordered their immediate execution and had their bodies flung into the nearby burn. When the waters of the River Wear rise, the 'lily of Lumley', dressed in a glowing white gown, is said to walk through the corridors and grounds of the castle, and there have been over 300 reported sightings of her over the years. Less conspicuous is a group of ghostly monks seen walking slowly along the path to the right of the hotel. Their silent procession ends abruptly when, having reached the castle wall, they melt one by one into its solid fabric.

SIZERGH CASTLE
Sizergh, Nr Kendall, Cumbria Ⓐ 🌿
THE STARVING SPECTRE OF SIZERGH

For 760 years, Sizergh Castle was home to the Strickland family, 27 generations of which filled the house with an array of priceless treasures before giving it to the National Trust in 1950. Inside are exquisite oak-panelled rooms, resplendent with intricately carved chimneypieces, and a famed inlaid chamber

ABOVE: The faded glory and weed-riddled steps of Sizergh Castle is an appropriate setting for a gaunt apparation who was starved to death by a jealous husband.

whose 16th-century plaster frieze, adorned with leafy scrolls and flower sprays, leads up to a sumptuously decorated ceiling. There is also a bedroom in which Catherine Parr may have slept when visiting her relations, the Stricklands, before becoming Henry VIII's queen. To find the origins of the castle's ghost we must travel back to the days when Henry II granted the estate to Gervase Deincourt, who built the pele (small square tower) around which the splendid castle would evolve. It was a violent age, when men dined with swords easy in their scabbards and with one eye permanently fixed on the border lest the whistle of an angry blade warned of the approach of marauding Scotsmen.

Gervase Deincourt was a particularly bold and ruthless warrior. His wife was famed for her beauty, and unfortunately, Gervase was an insanely jealous man. When he was called away to join the king in battle against the Scots, he locked his wife in a chamber, and told his servants that they released her on pain of death. Such was their fear of incurring their master's displeasure, the servants followed his instructions to the letter. As a consequence, the poor woman starved to death. Her gaunt wraith has haunted the castle ever since, a spirit caught in a fearful limbo between heaven and hell, whose anguished sobs echo through the otherwise silent corridors.

LEFT: The grim walls of Carlisle Castle enclosed the skeleton of a lady, whose ethereal reappearance once frightened a duty sentry, literally, to death.

ejected them soon afterwards. In 1745, the Jacobites captured the castle. Following the rout of Bonnie Prince Charlie's army at Culloden, many pro-Stuart rebels found themselves languishing in prison here and their cells can still be seen. From 1745 to 1959, it was home to the military, and today it is still operating as the headquarters of the King's Own Royal Border Regiment.

In the 1830s, during the construction of a parade ground and barracks, demolition work uncovered the skeleton of a lady bricked into a wall of the second storey of the keep. Three rings upon the bony digits of her fingers and remnants of her silk tartan dress were evident. There were no clues to her identity, although there was considerable speculation that she may have been walled up alive. The opening of her tomb, however, appears to have roused her revenant for, in 1842, a sentry on guard duty in the keep challenged the figure of a woman who approached him in the early hours of one morning. As she ignored him, he shouted to rouse his fellow guardsmen and then, raising his bayonet, charged at the figure. Just as he reached her, the woman simply melted into thin air, whereupon the soldier fainted clean away. Although his comrades did manage to revive him, such was the shock to his system that, having told them what had happened, he promptly fell back and died.

CARLISLE CASTLE
Carlisle, Cumbria Ⓔ Ⓐ
THE TOUCH OF DEATH

The mark of history casts a long and eventful shadow over the weathered walls of Carlisle Castle. In 1092, William II headed north and erected a castle, which 30 years later was rebuilt and enlarged by Henry I. Before it was finished, however, it fell into the hands of the Scots, before being recaptured by the English in 1157. It was later the home of Andrew Harclay, who was created 1st Earl of Carlisle after he intercepted an army led by Thomas of Lancaster, which he defeated at the Battle of Boroughbridge on 16th March 1322. Shortly afterwards, driven to despair by Edward II's inability to defend the north, Harclay entered into direct negotiations with Robert the Bruce, for which he was executed in March 1323. Over the years, the castle was used as a prison, its most famous inmate being the fugitive Mary, Queen of Scots, who was held here from 18th May to 13th July 1568. During the Civil War, the castle held out against siege from a Scots' army for eight months until, forced to exist on a diet of 'rats, linseed meal and dogs', the Royalist Sir Thomas Glenham surrendered. The jubilation of the occupying Scots was short-lived, for their former allies, the Parliamentarians, forcefully

MUNCASTER CASTLE
Nr Ravenglass, Cumbria Ⓐ
THE MALICIOUS GHOST OF TOM FOOL

This beautiful sandstone property dates largely from the 1860s, when the architect Anthony Salvin virtually rebuilt what had been the home of the Pennington family since 1208. Its elegant interior contains numerous treasures, but none is more prized than the so-called 'Luck of Muncaster', a gift to the family from Henry VI who, following his defeat at the Battle of Hexham in 1464, was found wandering on Muncaster Fell and was brought to the castle. The owners, Sir John Pennington and his wife, sheltered him for nine days. In gratitude, the king presented his

the lad to the castle on the pretence that Helwise was anxious to see him. He plied the boy with strong cider to render him senseless, and used the carpenter's own blunt chisel and heavy mallet to hack off his head. He then took the bloody trophy to his master, Sir Ferdinand Pennington. Today, the aftermath of the heinous crime still hangs heavy around the castle, and many is the time that the stillness is broken by the dull thudding sound of a body being dragged down the stairs. Occasionally this is accompanied by the mournful wailing of a woman, thought to be the grief-stricken cries of Helwise, lamenting her lost love.

The castle's Tapestry Room has a decidedly chilling atmosphere, and guests who have spent the night there have frequently reported bizarre occurrences. Some have heard the sound of rustling skirts as an invisible entity brushes by them. Others have been woken by the disturbing sound of an unseen baby crying. There are reports of a three-dimensional but very dark figure gliding towards astonished witnesses, which vanishes right before their eyes. Staff have long grown used to visitors approaching the door to the Tapestry Room and hesitating on the threshold as if fearful of venturing inside. Muncaster appears to have a veritable host of lost souls prowling its rooms and corridors, and perhaps John Ruskin's description of it as 'the gateway to Paradise' refers to more than just the beauty of the surroundings.

hosts with his gilded glass drinking bowl, promising that as long as it remained unbroken the Penningtons would remain at Muncaster. The cup or 'luck' remains undamaged within, and the Pennington family have retained possession of their castle for over seven centuries.

Another castle treasure is the superb portrait of Thomas Skelton, the 16th-century fool or jester to the Penningtons, who bequeathed the word 'tomfoolery' to the English language. A spiteful and vicious character, his master is said to have asked for his assistance when his daughter, Helwise Pennington, fell in love with the village carpenter. Skelton lured

THIRLWALL CASTLE
Greenhead, Northumberland ®
THE GHOSTLY GUARDIAN OF THE GOLDEN TABLE

Built around 1360, with stone taken from nearby Hadrian's Wall, Thirlwall Castle has stood in ruins for centuries, and time hangs heavy around its raddled walls. Yet those willing to poke about among the mouldering remnants might find something to their advantage. Long ago an owner of the fortress is said to have returned from a foreign war bringing with him treasure and jewels, the like of which had never glittered in these parts before, and most certainly have not done so since. Pride of place in this ostentatious cornucopia went to a solid gold table, which caused many servants to salivate with dreams of the wealth they could enjoy if only they could possess it. To ensure that they didn't, the master employed the services of a hideous dwarf, whose job was to guard the table with his life.

One day, a group of raiders arrived at the castle, drawn by local gossip about the splendid table. They put the garrison to the sword, and set about plundering the stronghold. But when they got to the room where the fabled table was supposed to be, they found it empty. They searched high and low but could find no trace of it. Furthermore, the dwarf had disappeared and, like the table, was never seen again.

According to local tradition the gold table still exists and is concealed somewhere within the hollow walls of the crumbling edifice. Indeed, it has long been maintained that, as the intruders were busy wreaking their bloody havoc, the dwarf spirited the priceless treasure into the murky depths of the castle well and, having leapt in after it, used his magical powers to seal his hiding place forever. However, those who come to this mysterious ruin seeking the riches that supposedly lie within should take close note of the exact nature of the taboo that the dwarf placed upon it. For he was most emphatic that the spell could only ever be broken by 'the coming of one who is the only son of a widow'.

OPPOSITE TOP: On a sunny day, the honey-toned sandstone Muncaster Castle looks welcoming, but I defy anyone to spend a night in the Tapestry Room!

OPPOSITE BOTTOM: Somewhere among these broken walls and rampant vegetation is said to be hidden a fine table of priceless value.

RIGHT: The high turrets that remain on parts of ruined Warkworth Castle, are a prominent landmark, although the castle is surrounded by houses today.

WARKWORTH CASTLE
Warkworth, Northumberland Ⓐ Ⓔ
HOTSPUR'S FAREWELL

Vast and unyielding, the dour bulk of Warkworth Castle looms above the surrounding houses like a mighty colossus, intent on subjugation. Built in the mid-1200s, every subsequent century has left a mark upon it, and the mighty ruin that greets visitors today is one of the most impressive examples of an aristocratic, fortified residence in Britain.

In the reign of Edward III, it passed into the ownership of the powerful Percy family and was placed under the command

of one of their most famous members, the redoubtable 'Harry Hotspur' (1364–1403). Having being captured by the Scots at the Battle of Otterburn in 1388, he was ransomed and later helped Henry IV overthrow Richard II in 1399. Hotspur inflicted a crushing defeat on the Scottish army at the Battle of Homildon Hill in 1402, and avenged his earlier humiliation by taking many captives. Henry IV's refusal to allow him to keep the ransoms for the prisoners led him to rebel against the king, and he was killed at the Battle of Shrewsbury in July 1403.

Today Warkworth Castle remains embalmed in the past. It is a place of shattered walls and dark corridors. The massive keep, with its high turrets, is visible from far around, and is little altered since the 15th century. Its lower floors possess a distinctly chilling aura, and dogs show a marked reluctance to enter them; if they do, they become decidedly alarmed. Children entering its dark interior have also been known to fall under its strange spell, becoming silent and contemplative – which, for stressed parents at least, can be something of a welcome relief!

CHILLINGHAM CASTLE
Chillingham, Northumberland
Ⓐ ⌨

THE RADIANT BOY OF CHILLINGHAM

Chillingham Castle is a dark and forboding place of twisting stone stairways, echoing corridors, creepy, dank dungeons and creaking doors. Its inner courtyard, resplendent with age-blackened faces that gaze down from the torch-scarred walls, is surely the most atmospheric of any in England. Its balustrades, pillars, balconies and romantic galleries could have come straight from the pages of Arthurian legend; and it would come as little

surprise if you were to encounter a knight in burnished armour, clanking his way up the sweeping stone staircase that delivers the spellbound visitor into the castle's sprawling interior.

Chillingham began life as a 12th-century stronghold. In 1246, the Grey family stormed it and evicted the owners. Their descendants have remained in possession ever since. Henry III stayed here in 1255, as did Edward I in 1298, en route to vanquish William Wallace who was making a decided nuisance of himself north of the border! Later, Sir Thomas Grey was given permission to fortify the family stronghold, and in 1344, Chillingham became a castle. Embellished and adorned by successive generations, the last of their descendants (by then the Tankervilles), moved out in 1933, and the proud bastion was allowed to fall into ruin. An aura of melancholic decay had soon descended upon the once mighty walls, as damp and rot chewed their way through the fabric. Then, in 1983, Sir Humphrey Wakefield, whose wife is a member of the Grey family, was allowed to take over the decaying ruin, and began a restoration that is still on going. Thus was the castle awakened from its long sleep. Visitors can now explore, and even stay overnight at, what is, without doubt, one of England's most guest-friendly and deliciously eccentric castles, devoid of the pretentious prissiness with which so many ancestral homes are imbued.

Several ghosts are known to wander the castle's eclectic and timeworn interior. The most famous is that of the 'Radiant Boy', a childish wraith that is seen in the castle's Pink Room, and whose heart-rending cries of either fear or pain echo through the corridors upon the stroke of midnight. In the past, the cries always seemed to emanate from a spot near where a passage is cut through the 3-metre (10-feet) thick wall into the adjoining tower. As they faded away, a bright halo of light would appear and the figure of a young boy, dressed in blue, would approach those sleeping in the room. Later the bones of a child, surrounded by decaying fragments of blue cloth, were found behind the wall. They were given a Christian burial and thereafter the 'Radiant Boy' was seen no more. Until, that is, Sir Humphrey began letting the room. Some guests complain of a blue flash that shoots out of the wall in the dead of night. Although they attribute it to an electrical fault, Sir Humphrey is quick to point out that there are no electrics in or around that particular section of the wall.

Another unquiet soul to stalk the castle is the spirit of Lady Berkeley, wife of Lord Grey, whose husband ran off with her own sister, Lady Henrietta. Lady Berkeley was left abandonned at the castle, with only her baby daughter for company. The rustle of her dress is sometimes heard as her invisible revenant sweeps along the rambling corridors, searching for her errant husband, and leaving a cold chill, not to mention unsettled witnesses, in her ghostly wake.

BAMBURGH CASTLE
Bamburgh, Northumberland Ⓐ
THE PINK LADY OF BAMBURGH

The subtle alchemy of sky and sea, swirling around the huge whinstone crag from which the fairy-tale turrets and lofty battlements of Bamburgh Castle rise, casts a potent spell that reaches far back into the foggy mists of time. It was once the ancient royal seat of the Kings of Northumbria, but suffered several attacks from the ferocious Norsemen. The last of these, in 1015, spelt the end of Bamburgh's days of glory. It was rebuilt, however, by the Normans, and following this, its lord, Robert de Mowbray, rebelled against the hated 'Red King', William II. Mowbray found himself taken prisoner, while his wife held the castle. King William brought the manacled de Mowbray within sight of the battlements, and sent word to his lady that unless she surrendered the castle forthwith, she could watch her husband's eyes being gouged out. Sensibly, she chose to surrender.

Besieged by the Scots during the reign of King Stephen and later bombarded with artillery by the Yorkists in the Wars of the Roses, Bamburgh was the first castle in England to fall to the power of gunpowder. It became a dilapidated ruin, until, in the early 18th century, Lord Crewe, Bishop of Durham, acquired it. Shortly afterwards it came into the possession of a charity run by Dr John Sharp, the curate of the village. Disturbed by the number of shipwrecks occurring in the treacherous coastal waters, Sharp established Britain's first lifeboat station here. In 1894 the first Lord Armstrong, whose family still own the castle, purchased it.

Needless to say, with such a rich and varied history, the castle has had ample opportunity to acquire a spectral populace that more than complements its mortal habitation. Several visitors have felt a spectral tap on their shoulder when on the flight of stairs near the library. Some have found it so unnerving that they have felt compelled to leave the castle immediately. Others have seen a misty apparition which they have unhesitatingly identified as being that of the village curate, Dr John Sharp.

Inevitably, the castle has also retained the spectral services of that mainstay of all castle ghosts, the female phantom in a coloured dress – in this case, pink. She has therefore become known as the 'Pink Lady'. At some stage in Bamburgh's eventful history, the flesh-and-blood incarnation of this forlorn wraith was a Northumbrian princess. Her father disapproved of the boy she was in love with, and sent the unfortunate suitor overseas for seven years. He forbade the couple to exchange messages and, hoped that his daughter's passion would cool. But the girl just became more and more depressed. In a last attempt to persuade his daughter to give up her love, the king told her that his spies had discovered that the boy had married someone else abroad. To cheer the girl up after this devastating news, the king asked the castle seamstress to make a fine dress in his daughter's favourite colour of pink. The distraught girl donned the finished garment and, climbing the stairway to the highest battlements, flung herself to her death on the rocks below. Shortly afterwards her lover returned from his exile, unmarried, and was heartbroken by news of what had happened. Legend does not record what fate befell him.

Every seven years, the princess's mournful revenant, clothed in a dress of shimmering pink, wanders through the corridors of the oldest section of the castle before gliding down the rocky path that leads to the beach. Here she stands upon the pale gold sands, gazing sadly out to sea, forever awaiting the return of her lost love.

Blood-drenched Walls and Demonic Fortresses

We have no title-deeds to house or lands;
Owners and occupants of earlier dates
From graves forgotten stretch their dusty hands,
And hold in mortmain still their old estates.

From *Haunted Houses*

By Henry Wadsworth Longfellow (1807–82)

SCOTLAND

T he ghosts that wander the corridors and historic rooms of Scotland's haunted castles are perpetual reminders of a stormy past. For centuries, this was a divided nation, its history spattered with the blood of countless conflicts, many of which were fought between the Highlanders and Lowlanders. Nowhere is this more evident than in the number of ruined fortresses and massive stone castles that stud the mysterious and enchanting countryside. They can be seen rising from the bleak desolation of the border with England, in the gentle farmland of the central lowlands, and set against the awesome splendour of the country's north-west corner, where wild and empty landscapes form Europe's last great wilderness. Behind the sombre walls of these impressive bastions, kings and queens, lairds and ladies, Highlanders and Lowlanders, continue to inhabit an ethereal domain. Many an old feud has never died, and dastardly deeds and ancient discords cross the centuries.

KEY

1. Hermitage Castle
2. Sanquhar Castle
3. Borthwick Castle
4. Balgonie Castle
5. Glamis Castle
6. Dunnottar Castle
7. Braemar Castle
8. Fyvie Castle
9. Rait Castle
10. Dunrobin Castle
11. Skibo Castle
12. Ardvreck Castle
13. Eilean Donan Castle
14. Duntulm Castle
15. Dunstaffnage Castle

HERMITAGE CASTLE
Newcastleton, Borders Ⓐ
BAD LORD DE SOULIS

Your worst nightmares could never conjure up a place as demonic as Hermitage Castle. It broods in desolate isolation amid some of the eeriest countryside imaginable. The warmth of a summer's day rarely penetrates its sullen bulk. Creepy corridors and cold stone staircases meander between the moss-clad walls of its ruinous interior, the very fabric of which seems imbued with a genuine ambience of menacing evil.

Built around 1300 on the disputed borderlands between England and Scotland, the castle's ownership would switch regularly between the two countries over the next 400 years, as the frequent conflicts that swirled around its towering walls led to its being dubbed the 'guardhouse to the bloodiest valley in Britain'. One of the earliest owners of

RIGHT: Jutting supports are all that remain of the floors inside Hermitage Castle, but the place still seems to echo with evil.

PREVIOUS PAGES: Many of Scotland's clan strongholds are in locations of ethereal beauty, such as Eilean Donan, built on an island where three lochs meet.

Hermitage Castle was Sir William Douglas 'the Knight of Liddesdale' who wrested it from the clutches of the Englishman Sir Ralph de Neville in 1338. Douglas was much respected in Scotland on account of his victories against the English. However, when Scottish King David II made Sir Alexander Ramsay sheriff of Teviotdale, the ruthless and envious Douglas lured Ramsay to Hermitage and imprisoned him in a 'frightful pit or dungeon, apparently airless and devoid of sanitation'. In this dreadful prison, he was starved to death, and his ghostly groans have echoed down the centuries ever since.

Most infamous of all the castle's bygone residents was Sir William de Soulis, who owned it during the reign of Robert the Bruce (1274–1329). Historically, Sir William was arrested and executed for plotting the assassination of Bruce in order that he might himself be crowned King of Scotland. Legend, however, has chosen to bestow a far more dramatic end upon 'bad Lord de Soulis'. Tradition maintains that this thoroughly evil individual was a practitioner of the Black Arts who kidnapped the children of the neighbourhood and used their blood in his sinister rituals, during which he would conjure up his demonic familiar, Robin Redcap. Eventually the local people petitioned King Robert, begging to be relieved from the scourge of their wicked lord.

'Boil him if you must,' replied the king, 'but let me hear no more of him.' Taking his words literally, the locals stormed the castle, wrapped de Soulis in lead, and plunged him headfirst into a boiling cauldron. His ghost now wanders the castle, a malevolent spectre, whose nebulous meanderings are often accompanied by the heart-rending sobs of children echoing along the crumbling corridors.

There is something strangely indefinable about this place, as if the malicious forces that are harboured within its vast, impregnable walls resent your presence. Indeed, it is easy to understand the local sentiments, recorded by Sir Walter Scott, that, 'The castle…unable to support the load of iniquity which had long been accumulating within its walls, is supposed to have partly sunk beneath the ground; and its ruins are still regarded by the peasants with peculiar aversion and horror'.

SANQUHAR CASTLE
Nr Sanquhar, Dumfries & Galloway ®
THE WHITE LADY AND THE MYSTERIOUS SKELETON

Sanquhar Castle, built in the 13th century and once a stronghold of the Crichton family, has long since fallen into ruin. It has a sad bearing, as though it can't bring itself to remember past indiscretions or acts of infamy. The chilling aura that descends as you enter is greatly enhanced by the knowledge that a golden-haired 'White Lady' is sometimes seen gliding around what little remains of the old castle.

She is thought to have been local lass Marion of Dalpeddar who, having set out to visit the castle in the 1580s, vanished

LEFT: Sanquhar Castle, a stronghold set in the charming landscape of Dumfries and Galloway, was the scene of a grisly find in the 19th century that shed light on the fate of an unfortunate female visitor in the 1580s.

BELOW: Borthwick Castle's twin towers and vaulted Great Hall make it a classic castle, and you can follow in the footsteps of Mary, Queen of Scots and stay there, too.

OPPOSITE: Balgonie Castle has a laird today who is happy to share his home with its past residents.

BORTHWICK CASTLE
Nr Gorebridge, Midlothian
MARY, QUEEN OF SCOTS IN PAGEBOY DISGUISE

Borthwick looks like a castle should – solid, resolute and defiant. Completed towards the end of 1430, it appears little altered since. Its massive twin towers, the walls of which are 6 metres (20 feet) thick, tower over you, looming and menacing, and it takes little effort to imagine the momentous events with which these walls are emblazoned. The upper section of the east parapet still bears the scars left by a bombardment of cannon unleashed against it when the then Lord Borthwick refused to surrender to Cromwell's forces. Standing between the two towers, you can imagine the terror of prisoners who were given the chance of freedom if they could leap the 3.5-metre (12-feet) gap with their hands tied behind their backs. Exploring the vaulted Great Hall, sitting in the tiny chapel, or absorbing the ambience of the comfortable bedrooms, it is easy to attune yourself to the vibrations of the past with which the very fabric seems to resonate.

In 1567, Mary, Queen of Scots, and her third husband, the Earl of Bothwell, fled Edinburgh and sought sanctuary within Borthwick's mighty bulk as the Scottish lords bayed for their

without trace. Rumour was rife that she had been murdered by one of the Crichton lords, possibly because she rejected his lustful advances. Whatever her fate, local gossip has always maintained that her remains were reposing somewhere within the castle. When servants began speaking of seeing her restless wraith gliding about the stairwells and corridors, it became common knowledge that she was returning to exact revenge upon the family. Indeed, it was soon noticed that her manifestations were always followed by tragedy or misfortune befalling the Crichtons. It was therefore something of a relief when, in 1639, the family sold the property and its ghost to Sir William Douglas of Drumlanrig. When he died, his family abandoned Sanquhar and it was left to fall into ruin.

Then, during excavations in the latter half of the 19th century, the castle gave up a ghastly secret. Workmen uncovered the skeleton of a woman, lying face down in a pit. It has never been established whether or not these were the mortal remains of Marion of Dalpeddar, though local tradition maintains that they were. The discovery of her tomb did nothing to deter Marion's spirit. Many are the wanderers who, while poking around the shattered walls, have felt an icy touch on the back of their neck and, turning round, have seen her fleeting phantom gliding around the ragged vestiges of her eternal prison.

blood outside. Bothwell, who knew that capture would mean certain death, made good his escape. Mary shaved her head and disguised herself as a pageboy. She climbed through a narrow window that can still be seen in the Great Hall, and lowered herself down by rope to make her break for freedom. She and Bothwell were briefly united. On 15th June 1567, he was defeated by the Scottish lords and fled Scotland. Mary fared little better, for she would soon cross the border into England and throw herself upon the mercy of her cousin, Elizabeth I. After 19 years of imprisonment, Mary was executed on 8th February

1587. Her ghost returns to Borthwick Castle, where she appears in the garb of a pageboy, her hair close-cropped, her wan features testimony to the stress of those desperate days.

BALGONIE CASTLE
Nr Glenrothes, Fife Ⓐ Ⓣ
SCOTLAND'S MOST HAUNTED CASTLE

The magnificent sandstone residence of Raymond Morris, the much-honoured Laird of Balgonie, is one of the finest 14th-century towers in Scotland. Probably built by Sir Thomas Sibbald, Lord High Treasurer of Scotland, it was added to and expanded over the centuries until David, 3rd Earl of Leven, built the final wing in 1702.

Despite playing host to several visitors of note – Mary, Queen of Scots, Rob Roy, Daniel Defoe, James Boswell and Dr Johnson included – the castle lay largely neglected by the 1840s, and letters began appearing in the Edinburgh press decrying its appalling state (not helped by the removal of the roofs to avoid paying the roof tax!). Throughout the 20th century, vandals and the elements hastened the castle's sad decline, and by the 1970s, it was little more than a melancholic ruin.

In 1985, Raymond Morris purchased Balgonie Castle; his family were the first people to live in it for 160 years. They soon became used to sharing their abode with the ethereal inhabitants to whom a fortress of such impressive antiquity is, inevitably, home. The laird's son, Stuart, has seen a ghostly old man walking across the courtyard; a head and collar materializing out of a wall in front of him; and a phantom dog

and its nebulous owner appearing, then disappearing, into an invisible doorway. One night, Margaret, the Lady of Balgonie, was asleep by the fire in the tower's upper room (the wind often howls in demented fury around the walls and windows, and there is no central heating!), when she awoke to find the figure of a man in 17th-century attire sitting on the sofa opposite. She looked him up and down and then, suddenly, he vanished. A few weeks later she came across a portrait of the 1st Earl of Leven, and immediately recognized him as the revenant she had seen.

The castle's most famous spectre is 'Green Jeanie', described in 1842 as being a 'well-known phantom'. Garbed in green, her face concealed by a hood, she wanders Balgonie Castle and has been seen many times in recent years. Nobody knows who she was, or what event, if any, made her such a permanent fixture in the castle's phantom guest book. She has been seen walking behind the iron bars of the ground-floor windows in the ruined 1702 wing and was recently captured on a digital photograph taken by a guest at one of the many weddings now held at the castle.

The Great Hall, which is the only room never to have been remodelled, still retains many of its original fixtures, and is imbued with a uniquely chilling yet tranquil atmosphere. It is a candlelit place of dancing shadows, where reports of indistinct shapes flitting around its darker recesses, or the oft-heard sound of disembodied voices engaged in muffled conversation, send shivers down the spine. Add to this several

'THEY'RE LIKE PART OF THE FAMILY.'

THE OWNER OF BALGONIE CASTLE ON HIS RESIDENT GHOSTS

cold spots detected by visiting mediums, an unknown 'something' that once ran its icy-cold fingers down the back of an astonished waitress, and a disembodied head that once floated out of the Great Hall – not to mention white and grey figures seen at several different locations – and you begin to understand why Balgonie has the reputation of being one of the most haunted castles in Scotland.

It is also a very spiritual and peaceful location, and the romantic chapel, bedecked in flowers and illuminated only by candlelight, is acknowledged as an extremely romantic wedding venue. The whole castle, cut off from the outside world by a huge encircling wall, seems trapped in a time warp, and exploring it in the company of the kilted and bearded laird is an experience without equal. Raymond Morris readily acknowledges the presence of at least nine ghosts at his home, but insists that none of them is malevolent. 'They're like part of the family,' he observes. 'They were here first; I just hope they're pleased with what we're doing here now.'

GLAMIS CASTLE
Nr Forfar, Angus Ⓐ
THE GREY LADY OF GLAMIS AND EARL BEARDIE'S OAFISH SPECTRE

Set against the stunning backdrop of the Grampian mountains, the soaring towers, lofty battlements and looming chimneys of Glamis Castle are both enchanting and

mysterious. It is the seat of the Earl of Strathmore & Kinghorne and was begun in the 15th century, although much of what survives today is of later date. Shakespeare would make Macbeth 'the Thane of Glamis', and set the murder of King Duncan within the castle's gloomy walls, although the slaying actually took place near Elgin. Much of the castle was rebuilt in the 17th century, when it acquired its French château look, and in the early part of the 20th century, it was the childhood home of Lady Elizabeth Bowes-Lyon, who would later become the Queen Mother.

At least six ghosts are known to wander its rooms and corridors. The scene of the first haunting is the atmospheric crypt, reached via a connecting door from the splendid dining room, which in an instant transports visitors from the stately opulence of the Victorian era to the more austere days of the Middle Ages. Behind one of the thick stone walls there exists a secret chamber, around which are woven many legends. It was here that one of the Lords of Glamis – 'Earl Beardie' as he was known – was once playing cards with the 'Tiger' Earl of Crawford. He was reluctant to give up the

ABOVE: The chateau-like appearance of Glamis Castle belies the fact that it is the legendary setting of Shakespeare's play of treachery and murder, *Macbeth*.

LEFT: The pathetic figure of a grey lady at Glamis Castle is thought to be Janet Douglas, who was unjustly condemned as a witch and burned at the stake.

game, even though the Sabbath was rapidly approaching. No sooner had the clock chimed midnight than the devil appeared and asked to join the game. The rash 'Earl Beardie' promptly gambled away his soul, and died soon after. For many years the ghostly sounds of cursing and swearing were heard echoing from the room at night and, in an attempt to quell the disturbances, the chamber was bricked up. But the foul-mouthed phantom could not be confined and his fearsome, bearded spectre is still said to roam the castle at dead of night; and there are several reports of guests waking to find him leaning over their beds, gazing at them with evil intent.

The castle's peaceful little chapel is the haunt of the Grey Lady, thought to be the ghost of Janet Douglas, wife of John, the 6th Lord Glamis. King James V hated the Douglas clan on account of the fact that he had been completely dominated by his Douglas stepfather and manipulated by other members of the family. Following the death of her husband, Janet married Archibald Campbell of Skipness and brought him to live at Glamis. King James had been waging a ruthless vendetta against the Douglas clan and, in what can only be described as an act of petulant spite, he turned his attentions to the popular and beautiful Lady Campbell and had her arrested on a trumped-up charge of witchcraft. On 17th July 1537, she was led from Edinburgh Castle, and burnt at the stake on Castlehill. Her ghost has been seen many times in the chapel, kneeling in silent prayer, a shimmering, translucent figure who exudes an aura of peaceful tranquillity and who melts into nothingness after a few moments.

Glamis Castle has many secrets, and its ancient walls must have borne silent witness to thousands of tragic and sinister events. Wandering its rooms, corridors and staircases, you can almost sense the eyes of past occupants

ABOVE AND BELOW: Small wonder that there's a sinister feel in the air at Dunnottar Castle (above) for it is where 'Braveheart' William Wallace (below) and his men slaughtered almost 4,000 Englishmen in 1296. And that is only one instance of multiple deaths there.

upon you, and it is easy to sympathize with the sentiments expressed by Sir Walter Scott when he visited: 'I began to consider myself as too far from the living and somewhat too near the dead'.

DUNNOTTAR CASTLE
Nr Stonehaven, Aberdeenshire Ⓐ
THE TEENAGE WRAITH

From its clifftop prominence Dunnottar Castle surveys the saw-toothed rocks that surround it with an air of almost arrogant indifference. The banner of power hangs around its walls, and it is one of Scotland's, if not Britain's, most impressively situated strongholds. William Wallace, the hero of the wars of Scottish Independence, dropped by uninvited in 1296 and, having captured the castle, killed 4,000 Englishmen here. The present building dates from the end of the 14th century, and was built by William Keith, hereditary Great Marischal of Scotland. In 1651, the Scottish crown jewels – the 'Honours of Scotland' – were brought here for protection from Cromwell's invading force. The Roundheads besieged the castle in 1652 but, because of its natural defences, it was eight months before they finally starved the garrison into surrender. The regalia, however, had already been smuggled to safety, and hidden in nearby Kinneff Church. In 1685, 167 Covenanters were imprisoned in a single room in the castle cellars during a long, hot summer. The conditions were appalling, and nine of their number died, although 25 others managed to escape down the cliffs. In 1716, owing to their part in the Jacobite uprising, the Keiths were forced to surrender their fortress to the government, and the castle became neglected. By the 20th century, it had become the dramatic ruin that is today, and external shots of

BRAEMAR CASTLE
Braemar, Aberdeenshire Ⓐ
THE GHOSTLY SUICIDE AND THE ENIGMATIC PIPER

Built in 1628 by the Earl of Mar, Braemar Castle possesses a charming ambience, and a ghostly lady, whose ethereal roaming came about as the result of a tragic misunderstanding some 200 years ago. One day, a newly married couple arrived to spend their wedding night at the castle. The next day, the husband awoke to a delightful spring morning, crept from their bed and went out hunting.

A little later his wife awoke to find him gone. Whereas a wife of some years' standing might view such an absence as a heaven-sent opportunity to enjoy a lie-in, this poor girl presumed that he had found their wedding night disappointing and abandoned her. Beside herself with grief and shame, she leapt out of bed, opened the window, and jumped to her death. Her melancholic spirit has remained trapped at the place of her suicide ever since. Witnesses describe her as a pretty young woman, with wispy blonde hair who appears whenever newly-weds visit the castle, no doubt intent on warning innocent brides that it is a common trait for the male of the species to disappear without leaving any clue to his whereabouts.

A Scottish piper appears in the castle's back corridor. An American visitor, thinking him to be a flesh-and-blood member of staff, waited patiently outside, hoping to take his picture. The custodians, noticing that she had been standing there for a considerable time, asked if she required assistance. When she told them that she was waiting to photograph their piper, they informed her that she might have a long wait, because he was, in fact, one of the ghosts!

ABOVE: An apparently solid, but actually insubstantial piper and a tragic bride roam the interior of the 17th-century Braemar Castle in Aberdeenshire.

it were used in the film version of Hamlet, starring Mel Gibson. Where Hollywood leads, the ghosts have been quick to follow. A girl aged about 13 years has been seen hovering around the brewery. She wears a plaid-type dress and has the annoying habit of simply melting away in front of startled witnesses. The spectral figure of a 'Nordic' man has been seen in the vicinity of the guardroom at the main entrance. There are places where a decided chill hangs in the air, and ghostly voices have been heard chattering in empty rooms. Thus this magnificent pile stares across the centuries contemplating past glories and infamies. It might not be the most haunted castle in Scotland but it is certainly her most haunting.

FYVIE CASTLE
Turriff, Aberdeenshire Ⓐ 🌿
THE GHOSTLY WRITING

Fyvie is one of Scotland's most magnificent castles. Its soaring baronial walls are crowned by five majestic towers, each, so tradition claims, a monument to the five families – Preston, Meldrum, Seton, Gordon and Leith – who, over the centuries, helped create this spellbinding stronghold of rambling corridors and splendid rooms.

Although now run by the National Trust for Scotland, Fyvie still has the feel of a family home, and the ghosts and legends that have collected both around and within its sturdy walls lend

it a definite air of mystery. The best-known spectre here is that of the 'Green Lady', thought to be Dame Lilias Drummond, wife of Alexander Seton, owner of the castle in the early 17th century. They had five children, all of whom were daughters, and this rankled with the ambitious Seton, who longed for a son. One day, his discontented eye fixed upon one of his wife's relatives, a young woman named Grizel Leslie. She was more than welcoming of his advances and, very soon, the two were enjoying a passionate affair. Neglected by her husband, Dame Lilias retired to their house in Fife where she became ill, and died on 8th May 1601. She was barely cold in her grave before Alexander Seton had married Grizel and brought her to live at Fyvie Castle. On their wedding night they were disturbed by

ABOVE: The five-towered Fyvie Castle is one of Scotland's finest, and bears on one of its window ledges, Dame Lilias Drummond's ghostly moniker, carved there to reproach a faithless husband.

moans and heavy sighs from outside their bedroom window. Seton comforted his terrified wife, assuring her that it was just the wind. But the next morning, on opening the window, he found etched into the solid stone of the outside ledge the name D LILIAS DRUMMOND. The mysterious impression is still there, while Lilias's spirit, swathed in green, makes frequent returns to the stairways and corridors of the old castle, bemoaning her betrayal, and leaving the delicate fragrance of

ABOVE: The 13th-century Rait Castle is a terrifying place to visit, especially if you know the story that goes with it.

OPPOSITE: The enormous Dunrobin Castle, in the far north of Scotland, possesses a 'ghost story with no ghost, and a ghost with no story'!

rose petals in her ghostly wake. In July 2002, an Australian visitor saw her in the dressing room off the Gordon Bedroom – where castle guides often complain of feeling that they are being watched A member of staff, who one winter's day was cleaning the castle armour, stepped aside to let a lady in a flowing dress pass by, and was astonished when she suddenly vanished. Another visitor was somewhat taken aback to see her reflection gazing through a green mist in a bedroom mirror. She is a harmless spectre on the whole, accepted as simply the oldest resident of this special and spellbinding fortress.

RAIT CASTLE
Nr Nairn, Highland Ⓡ
THE HANDLESS LADY IN THE BLOOD-RED DRESS

The ragged ruins of 13th-century Rait Castle are reached via a long and overgrown pathway. Its crumbling walls rise against a backcloth of woodland, and its sinister interior has been swallowed by a ravenous tide of creeping vegetation. It is one of the most frightening places you could ever wish to visit, and an overwhelming sensation of desolate apprehension seems to emanate from its very core. Perhaps it is the

knowledge that the Duke of Cumberland, or 'Butcher Cumberland' as he is remembered, stayed here on the night before the Battle of Culloden that imbues this unkempt ruin with its dreadful feelings of foreboding. Several different families have owned the property, but its singularly gruesome haunting is said to have its origins in an infamous event that occurred in 1524, when the warring Cummings held the castle. The then laird invited their arch-enemies, the Mackintoshes, to a banquet at Rait Castle, ostensibly so that the two clans could make peace. In reality, he intended to massacre them the moment they sat down to dine. However, his adversaries got wind of his dastardly plan, and having turned up heavily armed, they managed to kill several Cummings before making good their escape.

As his daughter was in love with one of the Mackintoshes, the laird was convinced that it was she who had revealed his plans. Furious at such filial betrayal, he chased the terrified girl to an upstairs room where, having climbed out of a window, she clung to the ledge by her fingertips. Her father hacked off her hands and sent her plummeting to her death. Whether he felt any remorse for his actions is not recorded, but retribution came swiftly when he and his followers were slaughtered, soon afterwards, at Balblair.

Ever since the ghost of his daughter has wandered the scene of her descent into eternity. Her handless spectre, resplendent in a bloodstained dress, is still occasionally glimpsed amidst the hollow ruins, a lonely vestige of a long ago day when, in dramatically taking leave of the castle, she left her mark on it forever.

DUNROBIN CASTLE
Nr Golspie, Highland Ⓐ
THE GHOSTLY SOBS THAT SHATTER THE SILENCE

More French château than impregnable fortress, Dunrobin Castle is, nonetheless, a majestic residence, and with 189 rooms is the largest house in the northern Highlands. It sits gazing out across the grey waters of the North Sea, and is one of Britain's oldest continuously inhabited houses, parts of which date back to the 1300s. The castle is the seat of the Earls and Dukes of Sutherland, and may well take its name from the 6th Earl, called Robert or Robin.

In the 15th century, the wicked Earl of Sutherland kidnapped a beautiful young daughter of the Mackay clan, and imprisoned her in what is now the castle's haunted room. He was determined to make her his wife, but she

steadfastly refused his advances and contemptuously rebuffed his proposals. One day, he came to her room and found her attempting to escape through the window by means of a rope of knotted sheets tied to the rafters. Drawing his sword, he sliced through the rope and sent her plunging to her death. In the past, her heart-rending sobs were said to echo from the room in the dead of night, although no one in living memory has heard her. However, in Duchess Clare's bedroom on the floor below (now the clan gift shop), ghostly footsteps have been heard pacing back and forth, and from time to time, the apparition of a man has been seen walking along the landing and disappearing through a closed door. Thus do the ghosts of Dunrobin Castle present the casual visitor with a spectral conundrum for, as the guidebook puts it, 'we have a ghost story with no ghost, and a ghost with no story!'

OPPOSITE: In the hope of gaining a larger and more imposing stronghold, the Laird of Ardvreck sought the Devil for his son-in-law.

BELOW: The romantic Skibo Castle was where Madonna and Guy Ritchie were married, but a former owner, as well-known in his day as they are today, met with a more sinister aspect of the place.

SKIBO CASTLE
Dornoch, Sutherland

THE RICH AND FAMOUS...
AND THE SKELETON IN THE WALL

Pop diva Madonna and film director Guy Ritchie chose Skibo Castle as the stunning venue for their 'showbiz wedding of the decade' on 22nd December 2000. Former United States president Bill Clinton dropped by for a round of golf. Visitors from all over the world come here to experience the ambience and opulence of a bygone era. It basks amid beautiful scenery and was once home to successive Bishops of Caithness, until the church relinquished ownership to the Gray clan in 1565.

Many decades later, a local girl is said to have disappeared after setting off to visit the castle. Rumours were soon circulating that she had been brutally murdered by the castle's keeper and her body hidden somewhere within the grounds. These rumours intensified when a ghostly 'White Lady' was seen about the castle and grounds during the hours of darkness, her wanderings accompanied by sorrowful moans and terrified screams. During renovation work, a woman's skeleton was discovered behind a castle wall. When the grisly

remains were given a formal burial the spectral activity ceased, but only for a time. In 1898, the Scottish-born American millionaire and richest man of his age, Andrew Carnegie, acquired the run-down estate and set about a rebuilding programme that culminated in today's lavish building.

Few could argue with Carnegie's description of Skibo as 'heaven on earth', despite the return of the fabled 'White Lady' who wanders its corridors and richly adorned rooms. Carnegie's grandson, Rosewell Miller III, encountered the White Lady one night as he was walking along a third-floor corridor. He watched her drift into one of the bedrooms, followed her, but found the room empty, and a subsequent search of the premises failed to reveal any sign of her presence.

ARDVRECK CASTLE
Nr Inchnadamph, Highland ®
TO THE DEVIL A DAUGHTER

The lonely setting of this picturesque ruin, once owned by the McLeods of Assynt, is haunted by the weeping apparition of a girl in white. She is reputed to be the daughter of a long-ago Macleod chief whose father entered into a sinister pact with the devil. Wishing to build himself a bigger castle, but prevented from doing so by lack of funds, the chief offered the Devil his daughter's hand in marriage in return for a new castle. The Prince of Darkness duly complied and the wedding was arranged. When the poor girl discovered the identity of

her bridegroom, she was so horrified that she threw herself from an upper storey of the castle. Her wraith has wandered the fortress ever since, weeping at her father's betrayal.

EILEAN DONAN CASTLE
Nr Kyle of Lochalsh, Highland Ⓐ
MIND YOUR HEADS

Alexander II built one of Scotland's most picturesque strongholds, Eilean Donan Castle, in 1220. It stands on an island at the meeting point of Lochs Duich, Alsh and Long, its ghostly image rippling in the silent waters, reflecting past eras of grandeur and mystery. Robert the Bruce sheltered here in 1306. Randolph, Earl of Moray, had 50 men executed here in 1331 and

ABOVE: The tranquility of Eilean Donan Castle and its surrounding lochs on a fine day are misleading: it has seen many a bloody bombardment.

displayed their heads on spikes. During the 1719 Jacobite uprising, William Mackenzie, 5th Earl of Seaforth, garrisoned the castle with Spanish troops (provided by a Catholic nation sympathetic to the Stuart cause)

Three English frigates, led by the warship Worcester, unleashed a bombardment of artillery against the defenders that battered them into submission, and left the castle little more than a mouldering ruin. It was rebuilt in 1932 by the MacRae family, and is now a clan war memorial and museum. The ghost of one of the Spanish troops who died in the bombardment is said to wander the castle, carrying his head under his arm!

DUNTULM CASTLE
Nr Uig, Skye ®
THE BRUTAL REIGN OF THE PSYCHOPATHIC CHIEFTAIN

The ruin of Duntulm Castle clings precariously to a commanding headland, gazing seaward. It is a deeply melancholic mass of crumbling, time-washed stone that was once a stronghold of the clan Macdonald. It is a place of mystery and intrigue, where legends abound and ghosts aplenty wander.

When the castle was a solid Scottish family fortress, Donald Gorm Mor, Chief of the Macdonalds of Sleat, imprisoned his cousin Hugh MacDonald for plotting against him. Not content with simply incarcerating his kinsman in a deep, dank dungeon, he fed him salted beef and fish, ensuring that no water was given to him. Hugh was driven to licking droplets of stagnant moisture from the foetid walls, and died a slow, agonizing death, his raging thirst driving him to insanity.

Meanwhile Donald Gorm Mor was busily scheming to add another infamy to the castle's dark past. His father had left him in charge of his ward, a one-eyed girl by the name of Margaret. She fell hopelessly in love with Hugh Macdonald and was devastated by the cruelty of his treatment. Donald Gorm Mor was incensed by the pity she had shown his adversary and made her life an utter misery. Driven from the castle by his vindictiveness, the heartbroken woman sought refuge in a convent and died shortly afterwards. Her ghost now returns to the castle and can be seen weeping among the

subsequent kings of Scotland were crowned. The present castle was erected in the early 1200s by the MacDougalls, Lords of Lorne, and stands four-square atop a rocky, commanding platform from which its solid walls appear to extend. The times were unsettled, and the clan enjoyed ownership for a mere 80 years before losing their fortress to Robert the Bruce. He installed Sir Arthur Campbell as the castle's constable, but, following Campbell's death in 1338, the castle was returned to the MacDougalls. It later passed, through marriage, to the Stewarts, who assumed the title of Lords of Lorne.

The chilly hand of doom weighed heavy upon the new owners, and in 1463 John, the second Stewart Lord of Lorne, was murdered by a renegade MacDougall, in the pay of the English. His brother, Sir Walter, inherited the estate. The succession was by no means a smooth one, for at the time of his death, John was on his way to church to marry his mistress and legitimize their son. Local sympathy was very much with the boy and resulted in six years of conflict. Sir Walter decided that the castle and lands were more trouble than they were worth and exchanged the lordship with Colin, Earl of Argyll, in 1470. His family, the Campbells, have owned the castle ever since and lived here until a disastrous fire in 1810. During the Jacobite uprising of 1745, government forces garrisoned it, and the following year it became a temporary prison for Flora MacDonald after her arrest for assisting Bonnie Prince Charlie.

The castle is still the seat of the Campbell Captains of Dunstaffnage, who spend one night each year in the gatehouse as symbolic occupancy. It is also the haunt of a lady in a green dress, said to be a *gruaghach*, a fairy or spirit woman, whose manifestations are closely knitted to clan fortunes. If she appears smiling, then they can expect good fortune to befall them. If she looks sorrowful, or as if she is weeping, the family can expect tragedy or ill luck to blight them.

ruins, while from deep beneath the ground come the clearly discernible ravings of Hugh Macdonald's parched revenant, proving that death did not end his torment.

Such was the castle's haunted reputation that later clan members found living here a positive ordeal, and so abandoned it to the elements.

DUNSTANFFNAGE CASTLE
Nr Oban, Argyll & Bute Ⓐ
THE FAIRY WOMAN

Embracing grand views of Loch Etive and the Firth of Lorne, Dunstanffnage Castle was once a stronghold of the Kings of Dalriada, the original Scots who migrated here from Ireland in the 600s. They brought with them the Stone of Destiny, which was later moved to the town of Scone, where

ABOVE LEFT: Duntulmn Castle, on its craggy granite precipice, was the scene of the Macdonald clan chief's cruel treatment of his cousin – that has resulted in disturbing events.

RIGHT: The sylvan setting of Dunstanffnage Castle is not enhanced by a fairy woman, for her appearances may bode ill for Campbell family who have lived there since 1470.

FURTHER READING

Abbott, Geoffrey. *Ghosts of the Tower of London*
(Heinemann, 1980)

Adams, Norman. *Haunted Scotland* (Mainstream, 1998)

Alexander, Marc. *Phantom Britain* (Muller, 1975)

Brooks, J.A. *Ghosts and Witches of the Cotswolds*
(Jarrold, 1981)

Brooks, J.A. *Ghosts and Legends of the Lake District*
(Jarrold, 1988)

Byrne, Thomas. *Tales from the Past* (Ironmarket, 1977)

Clarke, David. *Ghosts and Legends of the Peak District*
(Jarrold, 1991)

Coventry, Martin. *Haunted Places of Scotland*
(Goblinshead, 1999)

Coxe, Anthony D. Hippisley. *Haunted Britain* (Pan, 1975)

Curran, Bob. *Banshees, Beasts and Brides from the Sea*
(Appletree Press, 1996)

Dunne, John J. *Irish Ghosts* (Appletree Press, 1977)

Folklore, Myths and Legends of Britain
(Readers Digest Association Limited, 1977)

Green, Andrew. *Our Haunted Kingdom*
(Fontana / Collins, 1973)

Hallam, Jack. *The Haunted Inns of England* (Wolfe, 1972)

Harper, Charles. *Haunted Houses* (Bracken, reprint 1993)

Jeffery, P.H. *Ghosts, Legends and Lore of Wales*
(Old Orchard Press, 1991)

Jones, Richard. *Walking Haunted London*
(New Holland, 1999)

Jones, Richard. *Haunted Britain and Ireland*
(New Holland, 2001)

Maddox, Brenda. *George's Ghosts: A New Life of W.B. Yeats*
(Picador, 1999)

Marsden, Simon. *The Haunted Realm* (Little, Brown, 1986)

Mason, John. *Haunted Heritage* (Collins and Brown, 1999)

Playfair, Guy Lion. *The Haunted Pub Guide* (Javelin, 1987)

Puttick, Betty. *Ghosts of Hertfordshire* (Countryside, 1994)

Puttick, Betty. *Ghosts of Essex* (Countryside, 1997)

Seafield, Lily. *Scottish Ghosts* (Lomond, 1999)

Turner, Mark. *Folklore and Mysteries of the Cotswolds*
(Hale, 1993)

Underwood, Peter. *This Haunted Isle* (Javelin, 1986)

INDEX

ACKNOWLEDGEMENTS

So many people help with the compiling and writing of a book such as this. Librarians all over the country willingly looked up obscure facts and sent me necessary information. Custodians, guides and owners of the castles happily shared their stories with me and updated me on the current status of their hauntings. The people at Ryan Air and Holiday Autos did sterling work getting me about.

At New Holland I would like to thank Jo Hemmings for her unstinting support and encouragement and for believing in the project; Gulen Shevki for her evocative design; and Lorna Sharrock for her gentle chiding! I'd like to thank John Mason whose magnificent photographs are always so atmospheric.

On a personal level, I'd like to thank my sister Geraldine Hennigan who, as ever, was always there to proffer opinions and listen; my wife, Joanne, for putting up with my enforced absences and being so supportive, and my sons Thomas and William for all the laughter.

Finally, to all those whose stories and escapades have made this book possible: long may you wander, but may it always be in peace.

PHOTOGRAPHIC ACKNOWLEDGEMENTS

All photography by John Mason with the exception of those listed below:
Private Collection/Bridgeman Art Library: p. 39;
Royal Holloway and Bedford New College, Surrey/Bridgeman Art Library: p. 48; Britain on View: p. 122;
Fortean Picture Library: p. 76-7, p. 100; Hulton Getty: p. 114; Kristi Ormand: p. 109;
Mary Evans Picture Library: p. 75, p. 119c, p. 134t, p. 136, p. 144; Skibo Castle: p. 150.

(t= top; b=bottom; c=centre; l=left; r=right)